More Where the Ghosts Are

More Where the Ghosts Are

The Ultimate Guide to Haunted Houses

Hans Holzer

CITADEL PRESS
Kensington Publishing Corp.
www.kensingtonbooks.com

CITADEL PRESS
books are published by

Kensington Publishing Corp.
850 Third Avenue
New York, NY 10022

Copyright © 2002 Aspera Ad Astra Inc.

All Kensington titles, imprints, and distributed lines are available at special quantity discounts for bulk purchases for sales promotions, premiums, fund-raising, educational, or institutional use. Special book excerpts or customized printings can also be created to fit specific needs. For details, write or phone the office of the Kensington special sales manager: Kensington Publishing Corp., 850 Third Avenue, New York, NY 10022, attn: Special Sales Department, phone 1-800-221-2647.

Citadel Press and the Citadel logo are trademarks
of Kensington Publishing Corp.

First Citadel printing: January 2002

10   9   8   7   6   5   4   3   2   1

Printed in the United States of America

ISBN 0-8065-2219-4

Library of Congress Control Number: 2001092649

Contents

PART II

⌐

Introduction

~-

WHAT OR WHO are ghosts?
Ghosts do not travel: They do not normally follow people home; nor do they appear at more than one place. Nevertheless, there are some reliable reports of the apparitions of the dead having indeed traveled and appeared to several people in various locations. Such apparitions, however, are not ghosts in the sense in which I understand the term. They are free spirits, or discarnate entities, which inhabit what Dr. Joseph B. Rhine of Duke University has called the "world of the mind." They may be attracted for emotional reasons to one or the other place at a given moment in order to communicate with someone on the earth plane. But a true ghost is unable to make such moves freely. Ghosts by their very nature are not unlike psychotics in the flesh; they are quite unable to understand fully their own predicament. They are kept in place, both in time and space, by their emotional ties to the spot. Nothing can pry them loose from it so long as they are reliving over and over again in their minds the events leading to their unhappy deaths.

Ghosts have rarely harmed anyone except as a result of fear

found within the witness, in most cases because of his own ignorance as to what ghosts represent. On the few occasions that ghosts have attacked people of flesh and blood, as did the ghostly abbot of Trondheim, it was simply a matter of mistaken identity: Extreme violence at the time of death has left a strong residue of memory in the individual ghost. By and large, it is entirely safe to be a ghost hunter, or to become a witness to phenomena of this kind.

In terms of physics, ghosts are electromagnetic fields originally encased in an outer layer called the physical body. At the time of death, that outer layer is dissolved, leaving the inner self free. With the majority of people, this inner self—referred to by the church as the soul, or by others as the psyche—will drift out into the nonphysical world, where it is able to move forward or backward in time and space, being motivated by thought and possessed of all earth memories fully intact. Such a free spirit is indeed a development upward, and as rational a human being as he or she was on earth.

Ghosts, then, are very real, and the range of those who may at one time or another observe them is wide indeed. Anyone who sees or hears a ghostly phenomenon is by that very fact psychic. You do not have to be a professional medium to see a ghost, but you do have to be possessed of more-than-average psychic abilities to tune in on the refined "vibrations" or electromagnetic field that the human personality represents after it leaves the physical body. There are of course millions of people in the world today with this particular talent, and most of them not even aware that they possess it.

Ever since the dawn of mankind, people have believed in ghosts. The fear of the unknown, the certainty that there was something somewhere out there, bigger than life, beyond its pale, and more powerful than anything walking the earth, has persisted throughout the ages. It had its origins in primitive man's thinking. To him, there were good and evil forces at work in nature, both ruled over by supernatural beings, and to some extent capable of being influenced by the attitudes and prayers of man. The fear of death was, of course, one of the strongest human emotions; it is still. Although some belief in survival after physical death has existed at least as long as we have, no one has ever relished the notion of leaving this earth. To most of humankind, death represented a menace.

An even greater threat was the return of those known to be dead. In the French language, ghosts are referred to as *les revenants*—the returning ones. To the majority of people, ghosts are those who come back from the realm of the dead to haunt the living for one reason or other. I am still being asked by interviewers why such-and-such a person came back as a ghost. My psychic research and my many books published since 1962 have, of course, refuted the notion that ghosts are *returnees* from the land of the dead. Every indication drawn from direct interrogation of those who have had experiences of a psychic nature, as well as communications with the so-called "other side," has led me to believe that ghosts are not travelers in any sense of the word.

What exactly is a ghost? In terms of psychical research, as I have defined them, a ghost appears to be a surviving emotional memory of someone who had died traumatically, and usually tragically, but is unaware of his death. The overwhelming majority of ghosts do not realize that they are dead. Those who do know they are "dead" are confused as to where they are, or why they feel not quite as they used to feel. When death occurs unexpectedly or unacceptably, or when a person has lived in a place for a very long time, acquiring certain routine habits and becoming very attached to the premises, sudden, unexpected death may come as a shock. Unwilling to part with the physical world, such human personalities continue to stay on in the very spot where their tragedy or their emotional attachment had existed prior to their physical death.

Haunted houses, ghosts, apparitions and poltergeists are not the figment of overworked imaginations. According to parapsychology, the science inquiring into unusual phenomena of the human personality, sometimes the residue of past emotions remains in the atmosphere of a place. Sensitive people can re-create these emotions through their feelings and impressions. Many "ghosts" are in reality only imprints and have no life of their own. But conversely, many more are in fact split-off parts of human personality, remaining behind in a stage somewhere between the physical and the next dimension, unable to realize that their physical bodies have disintegrated and only their psyche remains to serve as the vehicle of unfinished business or unresolved problems. When the emotional pressure and frustrations reach great intensity, visual, auditory, and even three-dimensional effects are indeed possible; these are often reinforced by the physical energies of living people, especially those gifted with extrasensory perception, or young children before the age of puberty. The phenomena are then called poltergeists, or noisy ghosts. These can be quite upsetting, unless they are properly understood as desperate cries of a trapped human being in trouble, trying to reach out for salvation.

In this book, a sequel to my well-received *Where the Ghosts Are,* I have traveled to sites that harbor these unsatisfied energies. You may wish to visit some of them yourself to see whether any of them manifest for you. If you do seek out the places described in the following pages, keep in mind that a relaxed, open-minded attitude toward the phenomena is helpful. Patience is a must. What you search for unsuccessfully on a first visit might very well appear on a subsequent one. There are no hard-and-fast rules for success in the realm of a ghostly experience. It is only reasonably likely that someone will experience psychic phenomena in a haunted house if they are somewhat psychic. If one is highly psychic, then the chances are good that he or she will at least feel something of the unseen inhabitant of the place.

If you who read these lines are a complete skeptic and consider visiting haunted houses just a lark, remember an old quotation of uncertain origin: "I don't believe in ghosts but I'm sure as hell scared stiff of 'em!"

Even if you do not encounter ghosts or have a psychic experience in the houses described here, you will find them fascinating places. As locales for adventure in historical research, haunted houses have few equals. Whenever possible, take photographs using black-and-white film and time exposure. Something you do not see with the naked eye may very well show up on film.

Part I

ARKANSAS

Fort Smith and the "Hanging Judge"

—◆—

*I*F IT WEREN'T for the reputation of Judge Isaac C. Parker, called "the Hanging Judge," Fort Smith would be an interesting but otherwise unremarkable frontier fortification. Fort Smith was built in 1818 on a lonely and isolated spot in the Arkansas Territory where fighting often broke out between Osage and Cherokee. The fort was in part a secure stopping place for California travelers during the Gold Rush around 1849. In 1822, the Treaty of Fort Smith settled the dispute and safeguarded Indian rights in respect to white settlers pressing into the area from the East. Two years later, Fort Smith was abandoned due to changes in boundaries of the territory, and it was not until 1838 that the United States Army returned to the fort, mainly in order to stem the lawlessness that had become rampant in the area.

One of the most outspoken advocates of law and order at the time was Judge Isaac C. Parker, who went to Fort Smith in 1875 ostensibly to help restore order where outlaws had their way and Indians were often mistreated by the white settlers. In fact, Judge Parker had an eye out for justice for Native Americans, and he administered the law totally without bias.

Fort Smith and the "hanging judge"

Photographs courtesy Fort Smith National Historical Site,
National Park Service

Calling Parker "the Hanging Judge" is not entirely justifiable. During his twenty-one years as judge in Fort Smith, he did condemn 160 men to death for grave offenses, but only 79 were actually hanged. "It was not I who hung them," Parker said, "it was the law." Judge Parker's courtroom and the gallows are in tip-top shape today and can be inspected. You may even get a feeling of the intense drama that transpired here—if you have that "gift."

CALIFORNIA

The Ghost Monks of Aetna Springs

⌣

*A*ETNA SPRINGS is a little-known resort spot near St.
Helena, in Northern California. It is far to the north of
San Francisco and beyond the luscious wine country.
This very old-fashioned place consists of some wooden build-
ings as well as a good-sized golf course, and it has been visited
over the years mainly by older people.

In 1963, Dr. Andrew von Salza, a San Francisco–based physician, had gone to Aetna Springs for a brief vacation. The good
doctor, a camera buff, got to talking to George Heibel, the
owner of the resort, who owned a stereo camera, the latest thing
in photography at the time. Dr. von Salza asked to borrow the
camera, and the owner agreed. He took several shots with the
camera at midafternoon on a sunny day. Two of the photos
showed something neither he nor Heibel had counted on:
robed monks, enveloped in flames, walking on the empty golf
course! Heibel was shocked and immediately assumed that the
devil was playing tricks with his beloved camera, so he gave it
to Dr. von Salza as a gift.

When I visited Aetna Springs with the medium Sybil Leek
some years later, she spoke, in trance, of a group of monks

being persecuted by another group of monks. Sybil had not seen the pictures nor been told of their existence prior to our visit. She also spoke of the leader of this group, a monk named Hieronymus, who had been tortured to death here.

On my return to San Francisco and Los Angeles, I tried in vain to find evidence that a mission had existed this far north. The historical societies assured me there were never any missions or even settlements by monks in this area. But I was determined to uncover Aetna Springs' mystery. In New York I

The ghost monks of Aetna Springs, California

Photographs by Dr. Andrew von Salza

went through the files and storage bins of the Hispanic Society Museum and there, lo and behold, I found the answer.

In a Spanish broadside, a printed document not unlike a newspaper, dated 1532, the world was informed that a group of rebellious Franciscans had caused trouble way up north in California. They had learned that the Spaniards were abusing the Native American laborers in the silver mines of the area and complained about it to the Spanish Crown in Madrid. Far from being sympathetic to the injustices visited upon the poor Indians, the Spanish government alerted the Dominican Friars in San Francisco to look after the matter: meaning, of course, an Inquisition—that dreaded institution so often associated with the Dominicans. Sure enough, the Dominicans went to the northern territory, and they burned the Franciscans for their "rebellion."

Oh—the Franciscans were known as the Jeronomite Fathers, and the leader of the order was one Hieronymus.

The Queen Mary Ghosts

SINCE 1967, the great British ocean liner *Queen Mary* has been safely anchored off Long Beach, California. Now a prime attraction to visitors from all over the world, she has not always been a tranquil vessel. Stories abound about ghostly sightings onboard, starting from her maiden voyage, in 1936, through World War II, when she carried troops, and again afterward when she was once more a luxury liner.

Entire ships have appeared as ghost ships, from the mythical Flying Dutchman to more substantiated reports of ships that have disappeared into the sea and later risen spectrally above the waves. Most of these sightings are what we call psychic imprints from the past, rather than encounters with personalities with unfinished business. However, there are at least two stories of the *Queen Mary* that involve *bona fide* ghosts of real people, individuals hung up in space and time.

In 1966, a young crewman named John Pedder was accidentally crushed to death in doorway number 13 during a routine watertight-door drill. His ghost has been frequently observed and described in great and accurate detail by witnesses—down to the clothing he was wearing when he was killed. The second

The Queen Mary

Photo by Queen Mary Seaport Marketing Communications

case is that of a mysterious lady called only "the Woman in White." She makes her appearances in the *Queen*'s salon, and nobody really knows who she might be. But it is the young man in doorway number 13 who clearly needs help to "get across" to the Other Side.

The Winchester House

⌐

SAN JOSE, California, is more renowned as part of Silicon
Valley than it is for ghosts. However, right in the heart of
downtown San Jose exists a strange old house that, over
the years, has become a major tourist attraction for those visiting in the area. It is usually referred to as a haunted house—but
the ghost is the one who built it! The house itself is a crazy
quilt of annexes and additions to the main section, none of
which seem to make any practical or architectural sense. The
owner of this house was a lady whom I will refer to as Mrs. S.
She was extremely afraid of death, and after her wealthy husband died, she spent quite a lot of her inheritance searching for
ways to cheat death.

A psychic whom she consulted promised that as long as she
kept adding to her house, she would not be liable to die.
Whether the reader meant it seriously or as a joke, Mrs. S. took
it seriously enough to build year after year, avoiding contact
with the outside world as much as possible. Eventually, of
course, death caught up with Mrs. S., but there is evidence that
she has not left the house even now: It is widely rumored that
she now haunts the house she could never finish building.

The Winchester House

Photo courtesy California Office of Tourism

CONNECTICUT

The Curse of the Dudleys*

$\smile$

ABOUT TWO HOURS' drive from New York City, in Litchfield County, Connecticut, is the site of what was once a real town: Dudleytown. Now it is only a ghost town, and according to the late medium Ethel Johnson Myers, who lived nearby and visited often, there are also some real ghosts there . . . not just memories. So if you happen to visit this strange place and encounter a gentleman or lady of another time, don't be surprised and don't be afraid, as they all have plenty of problems of their own from the past and are unlikely to bother you much if at all.

Indians once hunted in the hills overlooking the present village of Cornwall Bridge, and owls—lots of them—used to live in the area's oak and chestnut trees. Because of their presence, the village acquired the nickname Owlsbury. In the middle of the eighteenth century, English colonists moved into the area. They farmed the land and prospered, and later the town became known as Dudleytown, after one of its founders. But the

---

*I am indebted to Dr. Karl P. Stofko, DDS, the municipal historian of East Haddam, Connecticut, for his help with this material, and that regarding the subject of the next section, Moodus, which now forms part of East Haddam.

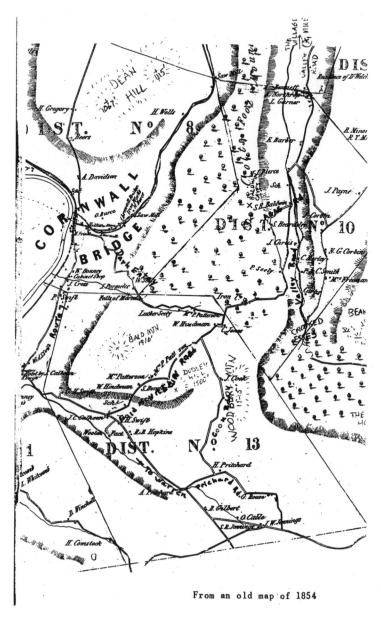

From an old map of 1854

Dudleytown

Photo by Paul H. Chamberlain, Jr.

good fortune did not last. Gradually settlers moved away, houses crumbled, and by the turn of the twentieth century, the town was completely abandoned. We have searched for rational explanations to account for this flight from the gentle hills of northwestern Connecticut. But the real reason for Dudleytown's fate doesn't seem "rational" at all.

When the first Dudleys arrived in the area, they perhaps should have known better than to be too optimistic about their eventual fate—but they had put an ocean between themselves and their past in the old country, thus assuming they were safe from the terrible *curse of the Dudleys*.

Apparently the Dudleys had angered the Tudor monarchs of England by siding with the rebels who had attempted to place Lady Jane Grey onto the throne. Both Lady Jane and her mentor, Lord Guifford Dudley, were quickly executed as Bloody Mary took the throne. Lord Dudley's brother, the Earl of Leicester, suddenly fell out of favor with Queen Elizabeth I and was forced to flee abroad for his life. One of his direct descendants, William Dudley, founded what eventually became known as Dudleytown, and the curse of the Dudleys had accompanied him to America.

Not only did this fearsome jinx wipe out the Dudleys, it also did in all those who tried to live in the accursed place: the Carters, the Greeleys, and even its last inhabitant, one William Clark, M.D. Dr. Clark had come with a plan: he had bought the ghost town as an investment, in defiance of the ancient curse. One day, as he returned from work in New York, he found that his wife had gone mad, for no apparent reason. That was enough for Dr. Clark. He locked up his house, took his ailing wife, and left, never to return. That was some eighty years ago, and that house, and the remnants of the town around it, have been empty ever since . . . except for the ghosts.

The Mysterious Moodus Noises

‌‌‌

"MOODUS IS a village in the town of East Haddam
[on the Connecticut River] and consists of a
small, nondescript shopping center, one remaining twine mill, and a small green surrounded by a few old
houses, a church, a library, and a school," wrote Dr. Karl. P.
Stofko, the municipal historian who also took the Moodus photographs in these pages. The map drawn by Dr. Stofko shows
how easy it is for East Coast travelers to get there.

What makes this place mysterious are the noises that seemingly emanate from way below the surface of the earth: rum-
bling, menacing sounds that have puzzled people in the area as
far back as the native Indians who once inhabited this part of
Connecticut. To them, the rumblings and accompanying earth
tremors were due to the god Hobomoko, who sat on his sap-
phire throne below and ruled over humanity. The name
Moodus comes from the native "Place of Bad Noises"—
Matchemadoset—which eventually developed into Machi-
moodus and was later shortened to Moodus. The disturbances
center around a hill called "Mount Tom" and a nearby cave,
which is said to be the entrance to Hobomoko's realm.

The Moodus Noises

Photo by Dr. Karl P. Stofko, DDS

Legend has it that a mysterious physician named Dr. Steel arrived in the area in the 1760s and settled on Mount Tom. Aware of the troublesome noises and the people's desire to have them cease, Dr, Steel assured them they were caused by a "great carbuncle" blocking the cave and that once it was removed, the noises would stop. Whatever the cause, Dr. Steel *and* the carbuncle soon disappeared—but the noises eventually returned to Moodus. Modern seismologists attribute the disturbances to local fault lines that cause small earth tremors from time to time. Personally, I prefer to think that Hobomoko is responsible.

FLORIDA

Fort Jefferson

BOUT SEVENTY miles west of Key West, Florida, is a group of small islands known as the Dry Tortugas. Today they are a wildlife paradise. In the eighteenth century pirates and smugglers used to hang out in the Tortugas because they were so difficult to reach from the mainland. They still are, but the trip is worth it. One of the islands boasted a very large prison fortification that in its heyday was called Fort Jefferson. Today the fort is an empty shell, but when it was built it was half a mile in circumference, and surrounded by a deep moat. Getting out of Fort Jefferson's clutches wasn't easy; it once resembled an American Devil's Island.

And that is precisely why the angry authorities dealing with the aftermath of the assassination of President Lincoln chose to send to this island prison a man whom they considered as guilty as the four conspirators who had been hanged. Dr. Samuel Mudd had become a convicted criminal for the sole humanitarian act of setting John Wilkes Booth's broken ankle! He had nothing whatever to do with the conspiracy, and he defended his action as something he would have done for anyone, even the devil himself.

Fort Jefferson

Photo courtesy Florida Department of Commerce, Division of Tourism

Dr. Mudd was to spend most of the rest of his life in Fort Jefferson, and his anguish no doubt still clings to the walls of his cell—psychic impressions of it can often be felt there. Recently his grandson petitioned the United States government to set aside the unjust conviction of his ancestor. Unfortunately, in March 2001, his petition was rejected by a U.S. district court. John McHale, a Mudd family spokesman, said that an appeal would be filed.

As many historians (this one included) know, the so-called conspiracy to assassinate Abraham Lincoln wasn't a southern plot at all, but was hatched and manipulated by members of the president's own government. Any show of leniency toward Dr. Mudd was most unlikely; the prosecutors displayed excessive anger and an apparent thirst for revenge at every turn—perhaps to divert any suspicion that might arise concerning their own involvement in the plot.

Fort Matanzas

～

*M*EASURING ONLY forty by thirty feet, Fort Matanzas in St. Augustine, Florida, would hardly deserve to be noted in these pages were it not for a terrible crime committed there. The fort was built in 1737 as a secondary fortification of ancient St. Augustine. The spot where it now stands had witnessed the massacre of the French Huguenot settlers who had claimed Florida for France in 1565. As a result of this treachery by the Spanish regional commandant, General Menendez, Florida became a Spanish possession.

The Huguenot settlers, who had been forced to flee from their native France because they were Protestants, had come face-to-face with the ever increasing and ruthless power of the Spanish conquistadors. Commandant General Menendez invited them to discuss problems of coexistence, or so he claimed. When the settlers showed up in good faith, he had them massacred by his troops. The killing of these "heretics" enabled Menendez to simultaneously serve two masters: the Catholic Church and the Spanish Crown.

A sensitive person may well feel the anguish of this long-ago event here, not likely to have faded away completely over the centuries.

Fort Matanzas

Photo by H. Milo Stewart III, courtesy Florida
Department of Commerce, Division of Tourism

Henry Flagler's Mansion
Palm Beach

✦

*H*ENRY FLAGLER was Florida's greatest booster—sometimes a hero to his people, sometimes a villain. Which attribution he was given depended on the eccentric millionaire's quixotic behaviors. As a partner of John D. Rockefeller, Flagler had made a fortune in grain and oil. After his first wife died, Flagler moved from Cleveland, Ohio, to New York with his small son. Soon thereafter he married his widow's nurse, Alice, and fired his sister Carrie, who had been acting as his housekeeper. On a vacation during the same period, Flagler "discovered" St. Augustine and decided to go into the hotel business there, first with the Ponce de Leon Hotel, which proved to be a raging success.

Just as he had "created" St. Augustine, making it into a fashionable resort frequented by the adventurous well-to-do, he then did the same for Palm Beach, where he opened the Royal Poinciana. In 1895, Flagler went to work to "create" Miami. Alas, Alice Flagler became ill and had to be confined to a mental institution. While his wife was firmly ensconced in her sanitarium, Henry Flagler met a young singer named Mary Kenan. Both he and his son were soon in love with Mary, an unfortunate coincidence that destroyed the relationship between fa-

White Hall, Palm Beach

Photo courtesy Palm Beach Chamber of Commerce

ther and son. Henry was able to divorce Alice even though she was institutionalized, by bribing the Florida legislature to pass a special law—the same law made it possible for him to then marry the youthful Mary Kenan.

In short order these scandalous events turned the people of Florida, who had once so admired Flagler for the prosperity he had brought them, firmly against him. He was forced to leave the state, moving with Mary to suburban New York. But his love for Florida was too strong to resist for long, and he decided to return. To regain his lost popularity he thought up a spectacular plan: He would build a railroad connecting the mainland with the keys, all the way down to Key West. And so he did. He was once more a hero, at age eighty-two. But he did not know that some thirty years later, after his death, a raging storm would wash his railroad right into the sea. Today, there is no railroad, but there is a causeway where it used to run.

Whitehall, his magnificent mansion in Palm Beach, is now mainly a museum. If you happen to get up to the top floor, under the roof, you may perhaps catch a glimpse of Henry himself. I have heard that he never really left his much-beloved Florida.

MASSACHUSETTS

Mysterious Follins Pond

*T*HE FOLLINS POND of today is a quiet inland lake on Cape Cod, Massachusetts, halfway between Cape Cod Bay and Nantucket Sound. It can easily be found by taking Route 6, which runs through the middle of the Cape. During the early Middle Ages, Follins Pond was not a pond at all, but an open inlet to the sea that ships could sail into from the open ocean. Thereby hangs the tale of Follins Pond, because it is here that the Vikings made their first landing in North America.

That the Norsemen had voyaged to America is common knowledge. Signs in the area point to sites of interest with names such as "Viking Rock," and though official tourism boosters make no claims to know exactly where the Vikings landed, many local people will tell you where to look for evidence.

In various parts of New England and Canada, remnants of Viking visitations have been found, but it was not until 1967 that the questions of exact landing places received renewed attention. A stone found near Byfield, Massachusetts, was deciphered and proved Viking presence in the area as early as 1009 A.D. Other authenticated stones were found as far west as

Follins Pond

Photo by Hans Holzer

Oklahoma, dated 1012, and some dated 1015 and 1022. The year traditionally accepted for Leif Ericsson's arrival in America is 1003. In his chronicles, Ericsson described an "offshore island"; explorer and author Frederick Pohl thought that it was not actually an island but part of the Cape, which is occasionally cut off from Nantucket by high tides. And Charles Michael Boland, an expert on Viking landings, believes that the site of that first landfall was on the Cape, and that the "island was no island at all, but an inlet of the sea."

Whatever the site really was, I wondered *exactly* where it was located, so I decided to try to pinpoint it with the help of famed psychic Sybil Leek. I brought her to Follins Pond, in my estimation the most likely site of Viking exploration. Not only did she verify my presumption (not knowing where she was or why), but she also spoke, in a trance, of a Viking longboat at the bottom of the pond. Her description of the boat, and the men she saw in the past, were both convincing and accurate.

Unfortunately, nobody has yet come forward to finance a diving expedition into the pond, so we can only hope that the longboat, and the shields decorating its sides, are still there, buried in the mud of what is now a pond, but was once an open inlet which the Vikings entered from the sea.

The Salem Witch House

～

*L*ET IT BE said from the outset: Just as there were never any "real" witches in Salem, so there weren't any in this house. But it did belong to one of the judges of the infamous witchcraft trial at the end of the seventeenth century, and, presumably, people accused of being what the Puritans believed to be "witches" were paraded in and out of it during the trials. As so much suffering no doubt took place in this fine house at 310 Essex Street in Salem, Massachusetts, it is quite likely that a sensitive visitor might sense that agony. This ability is called psychometry, or measuring an "imprint" from the past through one's intuitive processes.

The house at 310 Essex Street was built in 1642 and enlarged in 1674—twenty years before the Salem witchcraft trials. While there were no "real" witches in any way connected with the terrible hysteria that resulted in so many deaths of innocent people, there is nowadays a Wiccan coven and school headquartered in Salem, led by one Laurie Cabot, the self-ascribed official Witch of Salem. There not being any other, to the best of my Wiccan knowledge, her title is indeed secure.

The Salem Witch House

Photo courtesy Massachusetts Historical Commission

MINNESOTA

The Ghostly Usher of the Guthrie Theatre, Minneapolis

⤚

*L*OOKING AT the modern building that houses the Guthrie Theatre in Minneapolis, Minnesota, one would never think that it could have a ghost in it—except, perhaps, the thespic ghost of Hamlet's father.

A young man named Richard Miller, born in 1951, once worked as an usher in the theatre. He had been an avid skier but a serious accident on the ski slopes had left him with bothersome physical problems and prevented him from ever skiing again. He had gone to college but had not done well, and so had taken the ushering job. One night, the unhappy young man committed suicide by shooting himself while sitting in his car. Several years later, two young ushers were spending the night in the theatre to monitor the air-conditioning equipment. They were alone, yet they heard someone playing the piano onstage! When they investigated, they saw a cloudlike figure floating away from the piano. Several other ushers who also worked there claimed to have felt a presence or said they had seen smokelike formations.

One usher who often worked aisle 18, which was Miller's old aisle, was about to leave the theatre one night, the last one out.

The Guthrie Theatre, Minneapolis

Photo by Michael Daniel

When he glanced back at the empty theater, he clearly saw, standing next to the aisle, Robert Miller's ghost. On another occasion, a member of the opera troupe was crossing the parking lot to her car, when she saw a strange young man sitting inside the vehicle. When she challenged him, he vanished instantly. Her subsequent description of the unknown passenger fit that of Robert Miller exactly.

As the theater had been his only real home, it seems natural that the unfortunate young man would be attached to it unless or until someone were to help him leave and go to the Other Side. Say a prayer for him, if you visit there!

MISSISSIPPI

Magnolia Hall, Natchez

⟿

*B*UILT IN 1858 by Thomas Henderson, Magnolia Hall is one of the most spectacular large mansions erected in the area prior to the War Between the States, as it is called in the South. The hall not only boasts very fine furnishings and antiques, but the spirit of Thomas Henderson apparently still lives there too.

Some of the hostesses who show people around Magnolia Hall have reported the sound of footsteps in empty rooms; others have noticed indentations of a head on the pillow of the late Mr. Henderson's bed; and one visitor was adamant that he saw a misty appearance of the owner near the kitchen quite late one night. With so much effort and love poured into the building of this grand home, it is not difficult to understand the owner's reluctance to leave it, even in death.

Henderson was paralyzed before his death and could not speak. A local psychic believed that the mysterious footsteps and apparitions are his way of communicating after all this time. During the War Between the States, much military action took place here, from gunboat shelling to occupation by Union troops. The mansion is now owned by the Natchez Garden Club, but visitors are welcome.

Magnolia Hall, Mississippi

Photo by Magnolia Hall

The Waverly Mansion, West Point

BUILT BY Col. George Hampton Young in 1852, the Waverly Mansion is a splendid example of the Greek Revival style. Colonel Young died in 1880 and is buried in the family plot near the mansion.

After the Young family moved on, the house stood empty for many years. The dilapidated building was restored in 1962 by Mr. and Mrs. Robert Shaw, a couple from Philadelphia, Mississippi.

But apparently the original builder never quite left—and his presence is sometimes felt, though no apparition has been recorded. What has been seen a number of times, though, is the ghost of a little girl, probably a relative of the Colonel.

Sylvia Booth Hubbard, a chronicler of Mississippi ghost lore, has written about many houses in the state, including the Waverly Mansion. The Waverly Mansion has been designated a national historical landmark and can be freely visited for a reasonable admission fee.

We don't know if the child ghost is still there, but if you should visit there and hear a little girl calling plaintively for her mother, don't be alarmed. Instead, be gentle and explain that she has passed across to the Other Side.

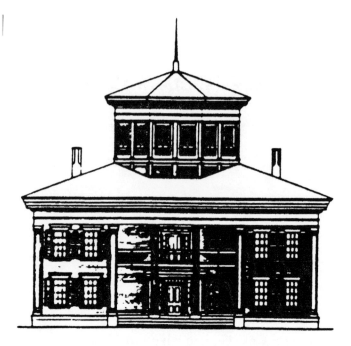

The Waverly Mansion, Mississippi

Photo by Waverly Hall

NEW JERSEY

Garrett Mountain:
The Revolutionary War
Never Ended Here

*N*EW JERSEY'S Passaic County boasts a rather remarkable parkland area, which the Park Commission rules with an iron but concerned hand from its current headquarters at the Lambert Castle, a nineteenth-century greathouse built during the Industrial Revolution by a wealthy businessman from England.

The park currently boasts relatively untouched woodland on both sides of a comfortable central road to the extensive parkland surrounding Lambert Castle. Entrances can be found at such colorfully named sites as Squirrelwood Road and Weasel Drift Road. To get there from New York, take Route 80 toward West Paterson, New Jersey.

In August of 1976, two young men named Victor Tartaglia and Joe Grosso were driving their car out of the park toward Weasel Drift Road around midnight. The park was supposed to be closed by then but one gate was still open. Rounding a bend, they suddenly saw a hunched, limping figure walking toward the same exit. As they approached the figure, their car lights shined right through the man, but they could plainly see that he had an injured arm and that he was wearing a Colonial soldier's uniform. When the light hit the figure, he turned toward

Garrett Mountain, New Jersey

Photo by Kurt Schuster

the car, putting out his uninjured arm as if to signal for help. They were quite close now and realized the man's body seemed to radiate and his eyes were like "glowing eggs," as they both said. That was too much for the boys: They stepped on the gas and sped out of the park.

When I heard about the mysterious goings-on, I decided to investigate personally and discovered that a Colonial military encampment had indeed been at the spot where Tartaglia and Grosso had experienced their ghostly encounter. I made arrangements to visit the park in the company of a psychic friend of mine, Kathy Koehler. The then director, Ronald F. Dooney, was most sympathetic to our quest and opened the gates for us after dark on April 28, 1994, when our party—and the ghosts—were the only ones about.

Kathy, who knew nothing whatever of the story, clairvoyantly described the area as it had looked in the eighteenth century. The man, she said, was named John James Cranston, the year was 1786, and the uniform he wore was that of the militia, not the regular army. Apparently, he had been knifed by an Indian fighter and had subsequently killed his attacker. Cranston had died of his wounds, but as is the case with ghosts, he did not realize he was dead. At the time the boys encountered the apparition, Cranston was evidently looking for help, not even aware of how much time had elapsed since his traumatic injury.

Since the area was fought over in many ways during the latter part of the eighteenth century, chances are that a sensitive person could reexperience some of the events that transpired there, perhaps running into a ghost or two. Mr. and Mrs. Kurt Schuster, and Cynthia Lightbody, two members of a New Jersey Parapsychology group, who visited the area in 1992, also "felt" the presence of a pre-Revolutionary identity there.

NEW YORK

The Angry Indian Chief of Amityville, Long Island

PICTURE THIS: You're a powerful Indian chief and, as is the custom, upon your death you are buried on your horse, upright, with all honors due you. Time passes, and one day there is a particularly heavy rainfall, which washes the soil away from the skull. Along comes a youngster who sees the skull, breaks it off, and plays football with it, not realizing what he has done. If you're that Indian chief, now supposed to be residing in the Happy Hunting Ground, you might be extremely displeased by this turn of events—so much so that you might just want to raise hell.

That is precisely what happened on the grounds of a certain Dutch Colonial house built at 112 Ocean Avenue in the town of Amityville, Long Island. The land on which the eighteenth-century house was built is part of an old Native American cemetery, but the builders didn't care.

The people who lived in the house never found peace in it—it has been the site of suicides, divorces, and people moving in and out for no particular reason. Then one day someone got the bright idea to move the old house elsewhere in town and, lo

Amityville, psychic photo by Gerry Wagner
Spirit of Indian superimposing on Dr. Holzer interrogating medium Ethel
Johnson Myers

and behold, all became serene for its inhabitants and has remained so to this day.

The real estate interests were not so serene, however, and in
1928 another house went up on the same site, roughly thirty
years after the Indian chief lost his head there. Eventually, an
Italian-American family name DeFeo moved in, but they were
not to find much peace there. The father, a religious man,
brought in a priest, who was subsequently driven from the
house by unknown forces. The lilies that were planted in the
garden died overnight.

Amityville House, 112 Ocean Avenue
Photo by Hans Holzer

Young Ronald DeFeo, eighteen, nervous and sensitive, woke up in the middle of the night one Friday the 13th, in November of 1974, took a rifle, and methodically shot to death all six members of his family. Upon investigation, no evidence was found that anyone had tried to escape, nor had anyone in the neighborhood heard any shots. But all six DeFeos had been killed by Ronny's bullets. Despite Ronald's claim to have no memory whatsoever of committing this awful crime, the prosecution obtained a conviction and Ronald DeFeo went to prison and is now serving a sentence of twenty-five years to life at Dannemora prison in upstate New York.

In my estimation, this case has all the earmarks of possession: an emotionally unstable young man, a family full of internal dissent, and a vengeful Indian chief bent on destroying anyone who dared live on his land. Building houses over Indian cemeteries is always risky business.

On January 15, 1997, at the request of the defense attorneys

Ethel Johnson Myers at Amityville

for Ronald DeFeo, I brought to the house a reputable trance medium, the late Ethel Johnson Myers. They hoped I might help to reopen the case on the grounds that their client, while guilty of murder, was at the time under the influence of the Indian spirit. But the lawyers were unable to persuade the authorities to reopen the trial, even though I saw DeFeo in prison and was convinced he was indeed in a state of involuntary trance when he committed the crimes.

After all the media attention, not to mention several books and three movies—two of them based on my stories—the new owners of the house, who had bought it cheaply and did not believe in the supernatural, were increasingly bothered by masses of curious tourists to the point of altering the street number on the house. Undeterred by this, the tourists continued to come. The residents were also bothered by an influx of self-styled investigators. These included a salesman from Elmhurst, Queens, who also called himself a Vampyrist; a team from Connecticut

Ethel Johnson Myers in trance at Amityville

Photos by Hans Holzer

consisting of a former artist turned "demonologist," his psychic wife, and a priest dismissed from his diocese; and even the occasional off-duty police officer.

Since I first began writing about the house in 1995, some amazing photographs have become available. Pictures don't lie—only people do.

Amityville can be reached by car, bus, and train. Ocean Avenue is easy to find once you arrive. But don't say I sent you. The current owner, a man named Wilson, doesn't believe in ghosts. He says all is well with the house. So far.

Raynham Hall, Oyster Bay

*T*HERE ARE actually two houses called Raynham Hall. The older one, located in Norfolk, England, was the ancestral seat of the Townsend family and is not accessible to tourists. A photographer there once accidentally obtained a photograph of the resident ghost, Lady Dorothy Walpole, which *Life* magazine published in 1937. The other Raynham Hall was built in Oyster Bay, Long Island, by an American branch of the Townsend family. It is now operated by the town of Oyster Bay and can be visited freely.

The ghost that resides in the American Raynham Hall seems to be associated with the Revolutionary War, when the British were quartered there. The phenomena often reported are footsteps and the feeling of unseen presences. During the war, Major John Andre visited Raynham, and one of his assistants, John Simcoe, had a love affair with Sally Townsend, the daughter of the rightful owner of the house. Local people suggest the ghost is Major Andre himself, but he did not die here. It is more likely that the ghost in Raynham Hall is the unhappy Sally: Not only was she jilted by the British officer, but her father broke with her over the affair.

Raynham Hall, Oyster Bay, New York

Photo courtesy Friends of Raynham Hall

The Deanery,
St. John the Divine,
New York City

～

THE CATHEDRAL CHURCH of the Episcopal faith in the
eastern United States is St. John the Divine, located in
New York on upper Amsterdam Avenue near Columbia
University. The building of this huge and impressive edifice
has yet to be completed, although American builders and arti-
sans from Europe have worked on it for extensive periods. To
one side is a smaller building called the Deanery, which is the
seat of the Cathedral Dean. It can be visited during normal
hours, and nobody need ask why you are there.

You might wish to visit the Deanery, however, not for its architecture, which is ordinary, but rather for its history—specifically because it's haunted.

My late friend Bishop James Pike was Dean of St. John the
Divine prior to becoming Bishop of California. During his
tenure at St. John, he was frequently disturbed by the sound of
footsteps where no one could be seen walking, and by what he
called "shuffles" on the stairs between the third and fourth
floor of the building, which housed the library and offices.
Bishop Pike's living quarters were on the third floor. When he
made inquiries regarding these phenomena, he was told that he

St. John the Divine Deanery

Photo courtesy St. John the Divine Library

had perhaps encountered the late Bishop Greer. Apparently, the reason for the late bishop's restlessness was his search for a very valuable pectoral cross, which had been given to him by Trinity Church and had somehow been lost. Some say the cross was shipped to Canada, but no trace of it exists to this day.

In 1980, I conducted a séance there with the help of the late medium Ethel Johnson Myers and tried my best to bring peace to the restless spirit. I did not hear of any further manifestations in the building, when I last visited it in 1997.

The Secret of the
Sonnenberg Mansion

NEW YORK CITY is home to Gramercy Park, a gated oasis of elegance and quiet. It is open only to the people living immediately adjacent to it, who possess keys to the park. The park is surrounded by lovely old clubs and genteel homes, among them a magnificent and well-preserved five-story Federal-style mansion built during the first half of the nineteenth century.

This property often changed hands and about thirty years ago became the property of a somewhat unorthodox proprietor, the very colorful and justly famous theatrical publicist Ben Sonnenberg. He cherished the mansion, lavishing so much money and effort on it that it became widely known as "the Sonnenberg mansion," even among the hoi polloi.

But eventually, Mr. Sonnenberg died. His last wish had been to be buried on the grounds of his residence. As this was slightly illegal (the cemetery lobby having done a thorough job years before), fulfilling his wish had to be dealt with prudently, and quietly. And so it was that Mr. Sonnenberg's earthly remains found their final resting place underneath the bushes, facing directly onto Gramercy Park. The exact location—that

The Sonnenberg Mansion, New York City
Photo by Hans Holzer

is, which bush he was buried under—remained forever secret. The Sonnenberg Mansion then went up for sale, and the contents were auctioned off separately, thus destroying the harmony between the house and its furnishings that Mr. Sonnenberg had spent so much money and effort to achieve.

In time the property was acquired by an Austrian baron, whose intention was to move his perfume company's headquarters into the mansion at some future date. Meanwhile, the mansion was under the care of a young couple, Mr. and Mrs. P., who occupied a small flat at the rear of the building.

Mr. P. knew of my work with haunted houses, and one

evening he telephoned me in an agitated state, asking me to come down to the property to investigate some strange happenings. It seems an attractive lady had appeared on the staircase and then disappeared quite suddenly, at a time when no one but he and his wife were about. They often heard footsteps, as well as doors being opened and closed. In short, all was not quiet on Gramercy Park. I agreed to investigate the mysterious goings-on, and so went to the mansion in the company of a psychic friend, Andrea S.

While I was taking photographs in the empty library, I suddenly "felt" I should look for a hidden wall safe. The surprised custodian, Mr. P., pulled back the drapes covering the French windows, and sure enough, there was a wall safe! I snapped a photograph of it while Andrea and Mr. and Mrs. P. stood behind me. When the picture came back from the lab, there was, unmistakably, a naked woman's arm extended toward the safe, as if to protect it. We feel quite sure that the arm belonged to one of Mr. Sonnenberg's late girlfriends.

The Sonnenberg Mansion has since become the property of famed fashion designer Richard Tyler. Whether he has yet encountered a ghostly protective girlfriend, I don't know.

A Haunted Dorm at
New York University

‿

T 110 WEST 3rd Street in New York City stands a frail wooden building that dates back to the early nineteenth century and once housed the stables of Vice President Aaron Burr.

The stable later became a nightclub called Café Bizarre. On the balcony that surrounded the back of the room, a group of young people reportedly saw the ghost of Aaron Burr observing the goings-on below. The then-owner of the club, the musician Rick Allmen, also attests to seeing the pale-faced man.

I conducted a séance at the site with the late medium Sybil Leek, during which Burr spoke through her. He told us how much he missed his daughter, Theodosia, who was lost at sea, and complained that history was treating him unfairly. He gave us further proof during our dialogue that he was indeed the late Aaron Burr and said that he had no intention of leaving the property.

The building has since had various owners and has recently been purchased by the neighboring New York University. NYU has decided not to restore this fine eighteenth century structure as a landmark but rather to tear it down and use the space to ex-

*Café Bizarre, formerly Aaron Burr's stable, a pre-Revolutionary building
torn down to make room for the Hall*

pand its facilities. Today it is the site of the D'Agostino Residence Hall. But ghosts, especially intransigent ones like Burr, never leave quietly. Residents often report seeing a pale-faced man in a ruffled white shirt popping up in various places in the dorm—and they are fairly sure he is not one of the students.

Filomen D'Agostino Hall, New York University

Photos by Hans Holzer

Washington Irving's
Sunnyside, Tarrytown

*W*ASHINGTON IRVING was a lawyer by trade, a writer by preference. He served honorably in the War of 1812, during which he befriended a fellow officer named Ichabod Crane. He found the name so humorous that he borrowed it for the fictional character that ran from the legendary headless horseman of "Sleepy Hollow" years later.

After the war, Irving turned down a number of government offers before eventually accepting a post as ambassador to Spain for four years. In 1835, he returned to his beloved Hudson Valley and bought an old Dutch farmhouse, which he spruced up to make it look more like a mystical retreat. He called it his "snuggery" and by all accounts he dearly loved living there. Irving died in 1859 and is buried in nearby Sleepy Hollow cemetery. Today the Irving house is maintained by Historic Hudson Valley, a nonprofit association, and is open to the public. It is only about forty-five minutes north of New York City.

What makes Sunnyside particularly interesting to me is different from what tourists usually hear about. Noises and footsteps in the house have been reported by several observers,

Washington Irving's Sunnyside
Photo courtesy Historic Hudson Valley

especially volunteer custodians. I visited Sunnyside with a competent psychic and filmed a segment of the NBC series *In Search of* . . . there. It seems that Washington Irving, purveyor of fictional ghost stories, was (and presumably still is) so enamored of his Tarrytown home that he does not intend to leave it. Not that he cares about the headless horseman outside: He knows where that one came from.

NORTH CAROLINA

Ocracoke Inlet, Where the Pirates Used to Roam

~

ape Hatteras, the treacherous stretch of North Carolina's Outer Banks was better known in olden times as "the graveyard of the Atlantic" because so many sailing ships were wrecked there. Perhaps because of the dangerous topography, which made pursuit by the forces of law quite difficult, the area was also a haven for pirates. Danger was always integral to pirate life and lore, and in the early 1700s, the rogues freely swaggered around Charles Town, terrorizing law-abiding citizens and literally getting away with murder.

Most notorious of these criminals was a native of Bristol, England, Edward Teach—better known to history as Blackbeard the Pirate. So brazen was this brigand that in May of 1718, he and fellow buccaneer Stede Bonnet blockaded Charles Town harbor, captured five vessels, and levied a fee upon anyone wishing to enter or leave the town. He got away with this without worrying about the authorities: Governor Charles Eden was his dear friend.

But eventually the local citizenry, and especially the merchants, got together to persuade the governor of Virginia, Alexander Spotswood, to help them get rid of Blackbeard. The

Ocracobe Inlet, North Carolina

Photo courtesy Clay Nolan/North Carolina Travel and Tourism Division

governor's men sailed out after the pirates, and after a fierce fight Blackbeard was shot to death. Lt. Robert Maynard, the commander of the foray, then cut off Blackbeard's head and took it as a trophy back home to Virginia.

Teach's Hole, beside the inlet where Blackbeard lived, is worth a visit. If you happen to see a headless pirate wandering there, pay him no heed: He's only a ghost looking for the rest of himself.

NEVADA

The Ghost Town of Rhyolite

〜

*T*HERE ARE haunted towns, like Dudleytown in Connecticut, discussed earlier in these pages, and then there are ghost towns, like Rhyolite in Nevada. Sometimes the two become one.

Overlooking Death Valley, Rhyolite, located four miles from Beatty via State Route 374 and U.S. Highway 95, flourished after gold was discovered there in 1904. At one time, three different railroads served the bustling area. But by 1910 it was all over, due to disappointing results in the gold fields, the havoc created among investors by the San Francisco earthquake, and the town's hostile natural surroundings. By 1920 only fourteen people were left in Rhyolite.

Visiting the remnants of what was once a thriving town with all kinds of attractions and amenities is a strange experience. As in similar places, those who have the Gift may just be able to tune in to some remnants of the past, and "hear" the voices long since stilled.

There are unused railroad sidings, stores long abandoned, and deserted houses. None of this has been removed, and no attempt has been made to salvage anything of value. The Ghost Town of Rhyolite is stuck in time; so are the emotions that once made it a hive of human activity.

The "ghost town" of Rhyolite

Photo courtesy Richard F. Moreno/Nevada Commission on Tourism

The Ghost Voices of Virginia City

⤚

VIRGINIA CITY is not only the location of the successful television series *Bonanza*, but a real historical town. In the 1800s the pioneers, the adventurers searching for gold, the cattle barons, and the lawless men of the West met and lived here.

Its once thriving social life is no more, but many of its buildings still stand carefully preserved. Among them is St. Mary's Church, better known as St. Mary's-in-the-Mountains. It was built in 1877 at the height of the Comstock Lode mining fever, and its bell is made of silver from that lode.

Visitors come to Virginia City all the time, partly because of *Bonanza*, and partly out of genuine historical interest. A few years ago, a group of curious students of psychic phenomena visited the church to investigate what had been reported by several witnesses.

Its seems that the witnesses, who were in no way interested in the paranormal, had entered the empty church on a quiet afternoon, only to hear the organ playing and a far-away sound of garbled voices. But there was no one about, and the organ had long fallen silent.

St. Mary's, Virginia City, Nevada
Photo courtesy Richard F. Moreno/Nevada Commission of Tourism

PENNSYLVANIA

The Black Bass Inn, Lumberville

━━

ESIDE THE Delaware Canal in Lumberville, Pennsylvania, not far from New Hope, stands the Black Bass
Inn. Built in the eighteenth century as a pub, it now
serves as a hotel. The place is filled with English antiques of
the period, as well as portraits of Kings Charles I and II, and
James II, which clearly suggests that the inn was once a
Loyalist stronghold. Today the Delaware Canal, which winds
around New Hope and some other nearby towns, is merely a
curiosity for tourists, but in the nineteenth century it was an active waterway for trade.

The story here concerned the ghost of a young man who
made his living as a canal boatman. Many years ago, the boatman died as a result of a violent argument with another boatman. After his death, his ghost had purportedly been seen by a
number of people over the years in the stone basement of the
Black Bass Inn. The current owner, Herbie Ward, had told me
their story, so I went to the inn to see if I could produce any
photographic evidence of the boatman's presence.

I took a number of photographs with fast color film in existing light. I also asked my companion, who had come along both

Black Bass Inn, Lumberville, Pennsylvania: Ghost of boatsman appearing to Dr. Hans Holzer
Photo by Rosemarie Khalil

as a witness and an assistant, to take a photo of me. You can imagine my surprise when the developed film showed a white shape in the picture which cannot be reasonably explained. By the way, the name of the boatman was Hans. Maybe he felt the two Hanses ought to get in touch. . . .

What's Not on the Tour
at Gettysburg

*I*N THEIR eagerness to simultaneously protect their environment and to serve a curious public, the commissions of national parks and important historical sites sometimes commercialize the sightseeing to a high degree. I am sure that most people are grateful for the fine-tuned itineraries, but to me these tours sometimes seem more like trips to an amusement park—and this is especially so for the larger historical sites around the United States.

Take Gettysburg, for example. You can tour the battlefield and the historical spots, everything neatly laid out on a map. More than two thousand markers tell you exactly where you are, what happened in that particular spot, and who was killed by whom. Anyone who leaves there and is not a convinced advocate of peace must indeed be hard of heart.

But the guidebooks and Gettysburg brochures are most unlikely to tell you that some observers visiting a spot known as Little Round Top, where one of the bloodiest phases of the battle took place, have on occasion seen a phantom soldier. Apparently, this soldier, unaware that he is dead, is searching for his regiment.

Little Round Top is not the only site in the area that is wit-

Gettysburg battlefield

Photo courtesy National Park Service

ness to strange events. Not far from the highway that leads to Harrisburg and on to Philadelphia is the rustic Graeffenburg Inn in Fayetteville. The Graeffenburg was named by its early owners after a spa in Austria, and there are medicinal springs nearby. It was built more than 150 years ago and has a charming restored Victorian interior, though its earlier construction is still evident.

The inn was brought to my attention by a student named Helen Forrest, who had been born there. Helen recalled to me that when she was five, she and her mother had both heard a woman singing in her room, though no singer could be seen. Helen's father managed the inn, and during his twenty-one years on the job, he refused to rent out Number 32, her childhood room. During all those years, a presence would open windows, move chairs, sing, and leave a definite lilac scent about. On several occasions, Helen felt the touch of unseen hands.

After her father died, Helen and her mother left Fayetteville. Subsequent managers were never able to make the inn

The Inn

Photo by Hans Holzer

pay off. Worse still, two of them were smothered to death—in Room 32!

Years later, Helen was working in summer stock nearby and decided to stay at the Graeffenburg, where she requested her old room, Number 32. That very night, she woke to someone shaking her violently. She saw no one and in panic ran out into the corridor—just in time to see the drapes catch fire and the bed she had just left burst into flames. Helen looked back into the burning room and clearly saw a small woman looking back at her. Then the flames took over. The room was gutted, but has since been restored.

What was the explanation for this sudden fire? The official verdict is that it was an electrical failure. But it may well have been caused by what parapsychologists call "spontaneous combustion"—in this case, due to an intense emotional presence. Whoever or whatever it was that shook her that night, Helen believes she is alive today because of the warning.

I made a trip to the Graeffenburg Inn, and I stayed in Helen's room in the hope that I would observe or sense some unusual phenomena. I took the accompanying photograph of the inn at night; as you can see, it is surrounded by a noticeably eerie glow. Nothing truly out of the ordinary took place while I was there.

The Logan Inn, New Hope

WHEN I DECIDED to spend a quiet weekend with a companion, Mrs. Rosemarie Khalil, to celebrate my birthday at the picturesque Logan Inn in New Hope, Pennsylvania, I had no idea that I was going to sleep in a haunted bedroom, but that I would actually encounter two ghosts for the price of one! The second encounter was in a nearby town in the Black Bass Inn.

The lady who communicated with us in the darkness of the silent January night, via a flickering candle in Room 6, provided a heartwarming experience. There was a definite feeling of a friendly presence in that room. If anything, being in a room so strongly filled with memories of another happy time only enhanced our own pleasure and relaxation.

The proprietor, Mrs. Gwen Davis, later explained to me that the ghost is the mother of a former owner, who simply liked the place so much she never left. I can only hope the visit helped the restless one acquire a better sense of still "belonging" to the house.

The ghostly lady at the Logan Inn is warm and loving, the sort of gentle spirit I call a "stay-behind." Unlike the unhappy

Logan Inn, New Hope, Pennsylvania
Bedroom

Photo by Logan Inn

chain-rattling ghosts associated with certain medieval castles, the stay-behind doesn't leave its old home because it is so strongly attached to the place in which he or she once lived.

Driving Into the Past on New Galena Road

～

*N*EW GALENA ROAD is in Bucks County, between Philadelphia and Doylestown, Pennsylvania. Perhaps one of my readers will someday experience something similar to the time warp encountered by two people who drove along the road back in the 1960s.

Time warp experiences are substantiated cases of physical contacts with people, places, and events in what I can best describe as "the living past," though the phenomenon defies all normal scientific explanation. These are not hallucinations; rather, they are three-dimensional experiences in the present, and seem to indicate that we still have a lot to discover about the nature of time and space—Einstein notwithstanding.

Now, back to the story of New Galena Road. On May 11, 1967, I was contacted by a reader of my books, Susan Hardwick of Philadelphia. She said that she wanted to share an amazing experience with me in the hope that I might be able to explain it. She told me that in the summer of 1960, she took a ride with a friend, Sal Sassani, along her favorite country road. Route 152 started outside Philadelphia as beautiful Limekiln Pike, which winds its way up to the mountains.

"I had traveled this road often over the years, and I knew

every curve with my eyes closed!" Susan explained. "About an hour after darkness fell, I sat up stiff, with a start: I knew we had not made a wrong turn, yet all of a sudden the road was unfamiliar to me. The trees were not the same. I became frightened and asked Sal to make a U-turn. As he did so, we both smelled what seemed to be a combination of ether and alcohol. At the same time, the car radio fell silent. Suddenly we saw a shepherd puppy running alongside the car. His mouth was moving but we heard no sound. Then, from our right, where there was no real road, came the ghostly shadow of a hearselike car; it crossed directly in front of us and disappeared. Then the odor vanished and the radio came back on at the same time."

I asked Susan whether she had had any other strange experience at the same location. She then told me about an earlier incident, which had not been as frightening.

"In the summer of 1958," Susan began, "I was driving with a friend, Jerry, on this same road, Route 152, and we turned off into New Galena Road. Halfway toward 611, which is parallel to 152, we came upon a wooden building I had never seen there before. We stopped and went in, and sat down at a table. Jerry noticed a man who resembled his late father, and this man addressed both of us by our names, calling Jerry "son," and telling him things only Jerry's father would have known. Jerry became convinced the man *was* his father. We left the building and drove on a road I had never seen before—yet I knew exactly what lay around every bend and curve! The incident took place about an hour from the city. I know exactly where this spot is, and I go by it now and then, but I have yet to see the structure or those roads again."

I decided to go to Philadelphia to investigate Susan's experiences. On July 24, 1967, the medium Sybil Leek and I met up with Susan and her friend Barbara Heckner. I had told Sybil nothing in advance about the case. As we were driving toward the area, I asked her if she received any kind of psychic impressions regarding it.

"This is not a ghostly phenomenon," she explained, "but a space phenomenon . . . we're going to cross a river."

We were approaching Lancaster, Pennsylvania, and no river

New Galena Road, Pennsylvania
Photos courtesy Bucks County Department of Parks and Recreation, and
William Mitchell

was in sight. Yet five minutes later, a river came into view. Sybil told us that she sensed masses of people in an open place, gathered for some reason; she compared her feelings to similar ones she had on an earlier visit to Runnymede, England, where people had once gathered to sign the Magna Carta.

Once we had reached the point forty miles from Philadelphia, where Susan had twice before experienced the inexplicable, Sybil again described what she was picking up on.

"It's a happening, not a ghost . . . in the past . . . two hundred years ago . . . *out of context with time* . . . I feel detached, like no-man's-land. We shouldn't be here . . . as if we were aliens in this country. I have to think what day it is, why we are here . . . it feels like a falling off a cliff . . . I feel a large number of people in a large open space."

When we began walking up an incline, Sybil indicated that the vibrations from the past were stronger there. "We are in their midst now, but these people are confused, too."

"Why are they here?" I asked.

"Unit . . . that is the word I get, *unity*."

I then turned to Susan and asked her to point out exactly where her two experiences had taken place and to describe them for Sybil. This would be the first time Sybil had heard Susan's story.

"But didn't you think there was something peculiar about all this?" I asked.

"Yes, of course we did," Susan responded. "Jerry's father had died when Jerry was a baby."

"Did everything look solid to you?"

"Yes, very much so."

"How were the people dressed?"

"Country people . . . work shirts and pants."

"Were the sodas you ordered real?"

"Yes, real, modern Cokes."

I looked around. There was nothing whatever in the area remotely resembling a wooden building. "You're sure this is the spot, Susan?" I asked.

"Definitely—we used to picnic across the road. That little bridge over there is a good landmark."

"What happened then?"

"We finished our drinks and left. When we got into the car, Jerry turned to me and said, 'That was my father.' He accepted this without any doubt. So we drove off and came upon a road that I had never seen before. I told Jerry there would be a dilapidated farm building on the left, around the bend in the road, and that there would be a lake on the right. We drove around and sure enough, there they were—just where I had said they would be."

"Did you ever find these places again?"

"Never. I am very familiar with the area. During my childhood I came here with friends many times."

"When you left the area, was there anything unusual about the atmosphere?"

"Yes," Susan responded, "it felt rather humid . . . but it was an August afternoon."

"Tell me what happened when you tried to find the place again."

"We retraced our steps, but the building was gone. The road was still there, but no building."

"Was there anything unusual about the atmosphere when you wandered into that bar?"

"Humidity, an electrifying feeling. It was very cool inside."

"Who was there?"

"The man who seemed to be Jerry's father, the bartender, and several other men sitting at the bar."

"Any signs?"

"Just signs like 'sandwiches' and different beer signs."

I thought about all this for a while. Was it a hallucination? A dream? A psychic impression? Susan assured me it was none of those: Both she and Jerry had experienced the same things; neither had been asleep.

"What about the people you met inside this place? How did they look at you?"

"Solid. They walked, and . . . that was the funny thing . . . they all stared at us as if to say, 'Who are you, and what are you doing here?'"

"When you first drove up here and determined that the area was unusual, did you notice any change from the normal road to this spot?"

"Only where the stop sign is now—that didn't exist. Instead there was gravel and that wooden building. It started right in from the road, maybe fifty feet away. Further back it was as normal as it is today. Suddenly I was there, and the next moment we were in it."

I decided to go on to the second location, not far away, where Susan's other "time warp" experience had taken place in the summer of 1960. As we approached, I again asked Sybil for any impressions she might have. She felt that "the strength of the force is again constant" between the two places. But she did not sense any of the odd excitement she had earlier picked up as we had arrived at the first location.

Once again, Susan pointed out the clump of trees as she remembered from the incident. "We were riding on this road," Susan explained, "which I have known firsthand for many years. It must have been around midnight, in the middle of July, in 1960. All of a sudden, this stretch of the road *became extremely unfamiliar.* The trees were not the same anymore—they looked much older than they are now. There were no houses here, just complete openness on the right side of the road." We could see a number of small houses in the area she was pointing out.

"This clump of trees was very thick," Susan continued, "and out there—where today there is no road—there was then a road. All of a sudden, on this road came a ghost car, like a black limousine, except that *you could see through it.*"

This was the same incident Susan had described in her earlier letter to me.

"How did the dog disappear?" I now asked Susan.

"He just ran off the road when the black limousine—a hearse, I'd say—pulled out in front of us. There is a cemetery right in back of us, you know."

As Susan and Sal were driving back in the opposite direction they had come from, the hearse was going away from the cemetery, not toward it.

"What about the driver of the hearse?"

"Just a shadow. The hearse went alongside our car and then suddenly vanished. The whole episode took maybe seven or eight minutes. We drove back toward Philadelphia, very shaken."

Now it was our turn to head back to the city. For a while we sat silent, then I asked Sybil Leek to speak up if and when she felt she had something to contribute to the investigation.

"I think if you stayed in this area for a week, you wouldn't know what century you're in," she suddenly said. "I feel very confused . . . almost as if we had entered into another time, and then somebody pushes you back . . . as if they did not want you. This is a very rare situation . . . probably a higher intensity of spiritual feeling. . . ."

I then asked Susan's companion, Barbara, to compare her current impressions and the ones she'd had on an earlier visit.

"An apprehensive kind of feeling came over me," she replied. "We were here again a week and a half ago, and when we came upon this side of the road, it was . . . different . . . it felt as if it was not normal. All along this run, as soon as we hit 152, through New Galena, I feel *as if I'm intruding* . . . as if I don't belong, as though this whole stretch of country were not in existence in my time. I've been out here hundreds of times and always had this odd sensation."

Susan Hardwick and her friends had never attempted to research the past history of the area where these peculiar incidents had taken place, but this is my professional bailiwick, so I was compelled to look into them further.

First I wrote to the town clerk at Traumbersville, Pennsylvania, because that was the nearest town to the area. I specifically wanted to know whether there ever was a village or a drugstore/bar/restaurant of some sort at the junction of Highway 152 and Galena Road, not far from the little bridge that is still there. I also inquired about the general history of the area.

The reply came on March 1, 1968, from the director of the Bucks County Historical-Tourist Commission in Fallingston, Pennsylvania:

"It is rural farm area now and has been from the beginning. From what I know about this area, and from *Place Names in Bucks County* by George MacReynolds, and Davis's *History of Bucks County*, I found out nothing about any drugstore in the area."

There was something else: Susan Hardwick reported finding some strange "potholes" in the road in the area. "They seemed like left from the snow . . . filled with water . . . like a whirlpool. We'd stop the car and put our hands into those potholes and *we could not feel the road underneath them.* We stuck our arms into the hole's, and got wet. But when we came back another time, there were no holes. No water. Nothing."

This puzzle sent me directly back to George MacReynolds's excellent work, *Place Names in Bucks County;* a source mentioned in the director's letter and one that I knew contained a detailed history of the area. And there I found at least a partial explanation for some of the unusual experiences along New Galena Road.

Back in the 1860s, galena and lead ore were discovered in this area, and mines were subsequently built. Soon there was a veritable mini-rush for prospecting for lead, and silver as well. People in the area began driving shafts into the earth to look for valuable ore underneath. (Those must have been the source of the "bottomless" water-filled "potholes" rediscovered by Susan and her friends—a kind of imprint from the past.)

By 1874 the fever was over, though another attempt at exploiting the local mines was made in 1891, and as late as 1932 some work was done to restore railroad tracks to the mines. But it all came to naught. "Today the place is deserted," writes MacReynolds, "a ghost of itself in the boom days of the 1860s and 1870s."

I suggest that so intense an emotional fervor as that of a small, backward rural community suddenly caught up in a mining fervor and dreams of great riches, might create a kind of psychic bubble in which the excited community continues to exist in a time-space continuum of its own, separate from the outside world . . . except for an occasional, accidental intruder, like Susan and her friends.

This theory helps to explain the strange perception felt by Sybil and Barbara that they were outsiders, and it may explain the water-filled shafts in the road. But it doesn't begin to explain Susan and Jerry's encounter with Jerry's "father" and the mysterious events surrounding that occasion. That explanation must await further research.

The Ghost at Oley Forge

~

ONE DAY IN 1975 I received a letter from Mr. Richard Shaner, a schoolteacher who lives in the heart of Pennsylvania Dutch Country. He inquired about my interest in his home there: "My wife and I live in a Colonial mansion built in 1750 by an ironmaster who was also a colonel in the American Revolution. We have reason to believe that a secret passageway was built in the vicinity of the mansion and that the home is possessed by spirits."

I promised to visit in order to investigate his concern.

Mr. Shaner's house and property, Oley Forge, was built originally in 1744 by Colonel John Lesher. The house stood beside Manatawny Creek, not far from Pleasantville, Pennsylvania, nearly equidistant from New York City and Philadelphia. Colonel Lesher had served as a liaison between the Pennsylvania Dutch people and Philadelphia, and he supplied General Washington's army with much material, some of it from his iron forge.

Over the centuries, Colonel Lesher's house became seriously run down, and Richard Shaner and his wife had bought Oley Forge in part to save it from vandals. The Shaners restored the

Oley Forge, Pennsylvania
Photo by Hans Holzer

old house with much love and, I am sure, much expense, so that they believe it now looks very much the way it did when Colonel Lesher lived in it. It is a two-story stone house on a flat piece of land, with windows reaching down to floor level. Near the house stands an old wagon of the kind that is still used in the surrounding Amish country, where many people have no use for the modern automobile.

To the right of the house is an overgrown area that was once part of the gardens but has since pretty much returned to nature. There are some remnants of slave quarters and other outbuildings that the Shaners have not yet had time to restore. On the other side of little Manatawny Creek and connected with the house by a narrow footbridge are the remnants of the ironworks. The area has been subjected to a number of archaeological expeditions by Mr. Shaner and his pupils. They have discovered a large number of artifacts, especially broken pottery, iron tools, and glass.

The house is furnished in eighteenth-century style, with many authentic pieces and some period reproductions. There are four-posters in the bedrooms; Pennsylvania Dutch chests, handmade and hand painted; and a long wooden table in the dining room; reminiscent of those you've probably seen in paintings of home life in the Colonial days. There is a spinning wheel in one of the bedrooms, and the only modern touches are the electric lights and the telephone.

"For miles around, people thought the house was 'haunted' for years before we ever got here," Shaner explained. "The place had always attracted me somehow. I wondered whether it might be possible to hold a séance in the house and discover something about its past. We decided to try it one Halloween—and I asked my students to try to find me a good medium."

I asked him what had happened.

"We had decorated the house with candlelight, and my students were most anxious about the whole thing. They had located a medium, Helen Terrell, who came all the way from Bethlehem, Pennsylvania."

Shaner went on to tell me that a while after the séance had begun, the medium said she saw a young woman in a long gown walking through the house, weeping because she was so happy that it was being restored. Then she described a well-dressed tall man coming into the sitting room and taking off his traveling coat. Next she "saw" a large dog with short hair, unlike any of the Shaner dogs, roaming through the house. Finally she described a man of very short stature walking through the center hall.

Soon after the Halloween night séance, Shaner received an inquiry from an attorney in New Jersey concerning Betsy Lesher, Colonel Lesher's youngest child. Apparently there was no genealogical record of her.

Sometime after receiving this letter, Shaner was lying half-asleep on his bed when he heard a little girl sassily recite a poem that she didn't know very well: "Twinkle, twinkle, little star, I wonder how you shine?"

Later, when Shaner undertook historical regression experiments with some of his students, he discovered that one of the upstairs rooms, now called the reading room, had possibly been used as Betsy's bedroom, which she shared with her grandmother. At a later séance, during which a hypnotist was also present, Mr. Shaner's brother-in-law, John Trout, served as a medium, and it became clear to him that the late Colonel Lesher himself was still around looking after his former home. Soon Shaner enlisted the help of some of his psychic students and the question of secret passages, and even treasure, came up. The teacher reasoned that since Colonel Lesher had been a wealthy man, he might well have had some secret hiding places in and around his home. So far, however, none have been found. I believe the search is continuing intermittently.

All in all, there appeared to be several stay-behinds from the Revolutionary period in Oley Forge, and if you happen to be lucky enough to be invited to visit, perhaps you might see, or at least feel one of them. The house is privately owned by Richard Shaner, but he is a friendly man, and if you come up with the right reasons, he just might invite you to come and sense for yourself.

SOUTH CAROLINA

The Mystery of the
Sorority House

⌇

THE ANTEBELLUM-STYLE University of Charleston is magnificently situated amid flowering trees and shrubbery. Located in South Carolina's major seaport, the university is an important seat of learning, and must surely have witnessed many a significant and dramatic event during its long existence.

Once, when I was speaking there, two young coeds took me aside and invited me to visit their room in the Knox/Lesesne House, one of the old homes near the campus that now serves as a sorority house.

Their room was believed by some to be haunted, which they thought perhaps would interest me. When I subsequently accompanied them and went upstairs into the haunted room, the atmosphere felt unusually cold and clammy, but no ghost made an appearance.

After I developed some photographs taken outside the house, something curious became visible in the picture: A female figure in white was quite plainly visible inside the window of the front-parlor room I had just left, *empty*.

On further investigation I discovered that during the Civil

University of Charleston, South Carolina

War a young woman had hanged herself in that front parlor. For reasons I was unable to determine, none of the students wanted to talk about the apparition, but I did ascertain indirectly, by talking to various students, that allegedly the ghost of the young woman had indeed been visiting some of them.

Haunted Room (Sorority House)

Photos by Hans Holzer

A Visit with the Gray Man of Pawley's Island

⤙

THE SANDY beaches of South Carolina's low country are beautiful and lonely. Just off the coast, not far from Georgetown, lies the sprawling Pawley's Island, named for Percival Pawley, who owned it many, many years ago.

Whenever there is approaching danger, such as one of the frequent hurricanes that plague this part of the coast, people sometimes see a strange, gray man standing or walking on the dunes. When they get closer, he dissolves into thin air. The Gray Man reportedly wants to alert the people to the approaching storm.

While to some this may be a charming legend, it is hard fact to the actual witnesses who have encountered him. Before a hurricane forecast in 1954, businessman William Collins, who fortunately refused to believe in ghosts, was walking the Pawley's Island dunes to check on the rising surf early in the morning. At that time, he was quite alone, or so he thought, until he noticed a man standing on the beach and looking out to sea. Collins assumed it was one of his neighbors who had also come out to check the rising tide, and so he called out to the man. When he got no response, he shrugged and went back in-

Pawley's Island, South Carolina

Photo by Hans Holzer

side his house. A subsequent weather report assured islanders that the expected hurricane had shifted direction and was unlikely to hit their area at all.

Collins and his family went to bed that night, unworried about the dangerous hurricane. But at five o'clock in the morning he was roused from deep sleep by a heavy pounding on his door. He could feel the house shaking from a rising wind: The hurricane had changed direction again and was about to hit the island after all. Collins went to his door and looked out. There on the verandah stood a stranger wearing a gray fishing cap, a common gray work shirt, and gray pants. Curtly the man told Collins to get off the beach to get away from the storm heading their way. Collins quickly thanked him and ran upstairs to wake his family. When he got downstairs again, just a couple of minutes later, the stranger had disappeared.

The Gray Man

Drawing by Catherine Buxhoeveden

After the storm had passed, Collins made inquiries about the kindly stranger who had warned him about the oncoming storm, but nobody on the beach had seen him. A highway patrolman on duty that night had not seen any stranger come or leave. Since the patrolman was watching the only access to Pawley's Island, the causeway over the marshes, the stranger could not have gone anywhere that night without his notice—once again, it seems that the Gray Man had warned someone on the island of impending disaster.

I visited Georgetown one Halloween some years ago to give a lecture about ghosts—what else? My hosts took me to look for the Gray Man the next day, a lovely, clear October afternoon. Pawley's Island looked peaceful and remote. But then, the Gray Man had no reason to walk for me in good weather.

Sightings of the Gray Man have been recorded since 1822. It is generally assumed he is none other than Percival Pawley himself, who could not leave his beloved island even in death. Some people, however, are convinced he is the spirit of an unhappy young man who drowned himself in the ocean when he found out that in his absence his fiancée had married his best friend. Whatever the truth may be, if you see him when you visit Pawley's Island, it might be wise to change your plans for a beach picnic.

VIRGINIA

The Ghost of the Hessian Soldier

~

*I*N THE ROLLING countryside near Charlottesville, Virginia, stands a beautiful, well-kept, small manor house of the kinds that helped make this part of the East truly outstanding historically. Built during the American Revolution, the house is now owned by a lady whom we shall call Mary, who at one time worked with Professor Joseph B. Rhine at Duke University, and therefore had more than a passing interest in parapsychology.

The oldest part of the house, which dates to 1781, is rather skillfully connected to the main house, and consists of a hall, a main room, and a small bedroom reached by a narrow winding staircase. The old part of the house has been the location of some very unusual happenings, which began so far as we know, when Mary acquired the house and acreage around it in 1951.

Whether earlier owners had had any unusual experiences in the house I don't know, as we had no way to talk to them. But when Mary had moved in, in 1951, she was emotionally keyed up—and perhaps this contributed to the experience that was to follow. One day soon after getting settled in her new house, she was in a small downstairs room that she had turned into a home

Last refuge of a Hessian soldier, Charlottesville, Virginia

Photo by Hans Holzer

bar, when she heard footsteps and a swishing type of sound in the main room. She knew that her husband was not home and the rest of her family was outside, so she called out to what she thought might be a stranger in the house.

There was no answer and the steps continued; Mary was certain someone was walking up and down in the room. She looked out the window and saw all her kids outside near the barn, evidently unaware of what was transpiring inside. Fairly upset by then, she summoned up her courage and went to find out who was there. She could not see anyone, but she could still hear the footsteps. They seemed to continue until they reached the doorway, then they went back across the room to the stairway and stopped abruptly at the landing leading up to the old room. At this moment Mary recalled a conversation she had with the previous owner, who told her that a former owner named Erly had once heard a strange noise, as if someone were falling down those stairs, yet upon investigating she had not seen anyone.

Two years later, in 1953, Mary's two daughters, then ages twelve and nine, were playing in the upstairs room while their parents entertained guests in another part of the house. At about ten o'clock in the evening they distinctly heard someone walking around downstairs in an empty part of the house. At first they thought it might have been a friend of their parents. They called out but received no reply. They didn't think too much more about it, but they asked their parents the next morning whether anyone had left the party to return to the main house. According to Mary and her husband, no one had crossed the covered walk that connected the two parts of the house; all of the guests had stayed in the main section.

Several years later Mary once again heard the familiar footsteps in the same area of the house. They would start, then stop again, then begin again. This time the incident inspired her to investigate the history of her old house. She discovered that the construction of the house began in 1781, and that there were three family cemeteries on the grounds. Before Mary bought the house, the fireplace had been rebuilt and at that time an inscription was found explaining that a Hessian soldier, a prisoner from a nearby barracks, had helped build that particular chimney in 1781. Mary found out that three thousand prisoners of war had been kept in a barracks nearby, mainly Hessian conscripts who had come to America against their wishes, serving with the British. Some of these Hessian soldiers had stayed on after the Revolutionary War and married local girls.

Virginia Cloud, a writer and very gifted amateur medium, knew of the odd goings-on there, and had told the owner about my interest in them. Virginia was able to get us an invitation, and we visited there together. None of the historical detail was know by Virginia when we got there. When we entered the house, she went into a semitrance state. Virginia described a soldier named Alfred or Albert, wearing a white shirt, boots, and trousers, and limping into the house, apparently because of a foot injury. Just as she was reliving the soldier's tale of horror, all of us heard a faint knock at the entrance door, and when we opened it no one was there. There is no doubt in my mind that the Hessian soldier, perhaps seeking some sort of last refuge, died in that house and somehow did not realize that he was no longer in his physical body.

The Ghost in the Pink Bedroom

A T ONE TIME the hub of the emerging young American republic, Charlottesville, Virginia, and its surroundings abound with haunted houses.

Before the American Revolution, large landowners built many magnificent manor houses that still dot the area, and much history and much tragedy occurred in some of them, so it is not surprising to find that reports of strange goings-on are comparatively plentiful around Charlottesville.

One of these beautiful houses, a historical landmark known as Castle Hill, is the property of Colonel Clark Lawrence and his family. The main portion of the house, of wooden construction, was built by Dr. Thomas Walker in 1765, and majestic brick additions were made in 1820 under the direction of the new owner, Senator William Cabell Rives. Senator Rives had been the American ambassador to France and his tastes were clearly influenced by French architecture and landscaping, as indicated by the entrance hall with its twelve-foot ceilings and the large garden painstakingly laid out in the traditional French manner.

On the main floor, to the rear, is a suite of rooms with a de-

Castle Hill, Charlottesville, Virginia

Photo by Hans Holzer

cidedly feminine flavor, the private quarters of Amelie Rives, a writer and poet whose body lies buried in the family plot on the grounds of Castle Hill.

Part of Amelie's suite is the pink bedroom, which is the center of some reportedly ghostly activities. Amelie herself spoke of a strange perfume in the room, which did not match any of her own scents. And many guests, who have slept there more recently, complain of disturbances during the night. The ghostly manifestations go back a long time, but no one knows exactly whose spirit is attached to the room.

From the testimony of various guests, it appears that the ghost is a woman, not very old, rather pretty, and at times playful. Her intentions seem to be to frighten most people. Curiously, however, a few guests have slept in the Pink

Bedroom undisturbed. Legend has it that those the lady ghost likes may sleep peacefully in "her" bedroom, while those she does not like must be frightened out of their wits.

I visited the Pink Bedroom in the company of sensitive Virginia Cloud, who had been there many times, and I felt the vibrations of another presence, a fine, almost gentle person, but I could not see anyone. Nevertheless, I realized that I was not alone in the room, and Miss Cloud also felt that we were probably being observed by an unseen former owner.

During the Revolutionary War, British General Banastre Tarleton and his troops occupied Castle Hill. Dr. Walker, whose home it was then, served them breakfast on June 4, 1781, and in the course of his hospitality delayed them as long as he could so that Jefferson, in nearby Charlottesville, could make good his escape from the British. Whether one of the ladies who lived there played any significant part in this delaying action is not known, but my suspicion is that there was indeed involvement of that kind and that it is connected with the appearance of the ghostly lady at Castle Hill. It was not uncommmon for the women of the Colonial period to use their charms on the British, in order to further the cause of the Revolution. Although Castle Hill is not open to visitors—especially those searching for the ghost—it is conceivable that a "student of history" could diplomatically arrange for a brief visit.

TEXAS

The Alamo, San Antonio

—◡—

*T*HE ALAMO, as every American schoolchild knows, was a
mission-fortress meant to defend the city of San Antonio
against Mexico, its enemy directly to the south.

In 1836, the Mexican general and president Santa Anna laid
siege to the Alamo, and most of its defenders died in the ensu-
ing battle.

But just prior to the final onslaught, in January of 1836, the
defenders placed their most valuable possessions and personal
mementos inside one of the mission's bells. Then the bell was
hidden at the bottom of a deep well. All sorts of stories are still
told about what lies buried underneath the Alamo, including
treasure, silver, and gold, and a private group called the Tesoro
de Alamo Preservation Sociate has been digging for it since
1995. They have indeed found some interesting artifacts, but
from an earlier period.

Modern visitors to the historic fort report encountering a
ghost on the top of the Alamo, walking to and fro along the wall
as if in search of an escape.

Since the purported treasure has not yet been found, perhaps
this ghost is guarding it still.

The Alamo

Photo by Cheryl Hanzi

WASHINGTON, D.C.

The Woodrow Wilson House

*L*OCATED AT 2340 S Street in the nation's capital, the Woodrow Wilson House was built in 1915. In 1920, toward the end of his second term in office, President Wilson and his second wife, Edith Bolling Wilson, acquired it as a residence. Wilson died in 1924, and when Mrs. Wilson died in 1961, their house came under the wing of the National Trust. It is now a museum dedicated to the Wilson presidency.

Rumors of psychic phenomena continue to circulate around this house and date back to Mrs. Wilson's passing. In 1969, Jose Vasquez, the caretaker, witnessed a phenomenon he could not explain. "Someone" was standing behind him when he played the piano downstairs. In the president's bedroom upstairs, loud footsteps were clearly audible, yet nobody could be seen walking. Something, or someone, from the spirit world seemed to be quite active in the Woodrow Wilson House, and when word got to me about it, I took the late medium Ethel Johnson Myers with me to Washington. In the séance with her that followed, President Wilson spoke through her while she was in deep trance, talking about his struggle for the brotherhood of man,

The Woodrow Wilson House, Washington, D.C.

Photo courtesy Woodrow Wilson House

and looking forward to the year when enemies would join hands for world peace. This he foresaw happening in 1989.

In 1989, the soviet Union went out of business, and relations thawed between Russia and the United States. Remember, Mr. Wilson foretold this in 1969!

CANADA

The Mackenzie House, Toronto

⌇

*T*HE MACKENZIE HOUSE, at 82 Bond Street in downtown Toronto, was home of the first mayor of Toronto, William Lyon Mackenzie.

A strong sense of gloom has been reported by many visitors in the bedroom where the mayor died in 1861.

Until fairly recently, the house was an adjunct office to the Canadian Broadcasting Corporation (CBC), serving as headquarters for its radio network. After several caretakers complained about the presence of ghosts in the offices, the Canadian Broadcasting Corporation took the unusual step of calling in a minister, the Canon C. J. Frank, to try to exorcise any spirits there might be. Since Canon Frank could not locate a formal exorcism text, he made up an appropriate prayer for the souls of the earthbound spirits in the place. The local specialist on ghost lore, and a fine television host and reporter, Eileen Sonin, revisited the house after the exorcism and found the atmosphere there to be much calmer.

The CBC also owned a building at 90 Sumach Street, but has given up its interest there. On the fourth floor of that building,

The Mackenzie House, Toronto

Photo courtesy Tourism Toronto

the ghost of a thin man dressed in black has been seen near the elevator. Eileen Sonin believes that this specter is connected to an event that occurred in a brewery that stood on the same site before the present building. One of the brewery workers had died in an explosion there at the turn of the century—on the fourth floor!

Both buildings can be visited without difficulty.

The Ghost at Toronto
University

⌒

HEN SIR ALAN AYLESWORTH, a well-known Toronto personality, was a student at Toronto University, he met a stranger in what is called the Arcade of the Cloisters. Aylesworth was intrigued by the man, who said his name was Ivan Reznikoff, and invited him to his residence for a drink. The stranger told his host that he was a stonemason by trade and that he had worked on the building of the college.

And here the story becomes quite curious. The stranger maintained that he and another stonemason had fought fiercely with knives atop the central tower. There were quarreling over a girl, and Reznikoff said that he himself had been stabbed to death and thrown down from the tower.

And Aylesworth is not the only one who has seen a "ghost"— if that is what he saw—in the same vicinity. In 1866, a registrar named Falconbridge encountered an apparition that he described as a bearded man wearing a comical hat. Another witness, Beadle McKim, reported seeing the same ghost near the main tower; when McKim challenged him, the figure immediately vanished. And reported sightings continue to this day, most often in the same college area, known as the Arcades.

Toronto University

Photo courtesy Tourism Toronto

After a fire at the university in 1890, a human skull, some human bones, and a belt buckle were found at the bottom of the tower well, according to the account researched by Eileen Sonin.

Could those have been the bones of Ivan Reznikoff?

Part II

MYSTERY HILL

Mystery Hill

PSYCHOMETRIC "time travel" often includes encounters with ghosts. It is often difficult to distinguish between the two experiences but if the people one encounters are responding to the visitor in some fashion, they are clearly not just imprints from the past but people who have remained behind either by choice or by emotional, compelling ties to the spot.

One of these places is Mystery Hill, popularly called "the American Stonehenge," in North Salem, New Hampshire.

People visiting there—and not just psychics—have reported encountering people from the past, and since such experiences can happen to anyone who has the psychic gift, I thought including the case of the American Stonehenge would be helpful.

The hill on which it stands, or rather what is left of it, is a major tourist attraction. The private society, which was responsible for the archeological work, dubbed it Mystery Hill, although we have uncovered part of the mystery. We know now that ancient seafaring people came there long before Columbus, long before anyone else.

The Mystery of Mystery Hill
North Salem, New Hampshire

*I*N A RECENT work called *Long Before Columbus/How the Ancients Discovered America*, I spoke of a remarkable ruin on a hill near Salem, New Hampshire, popularly known as Mystery Hill.

Scientific investigations by reputable researchers were able to prove that the observatory, which so very much reminded one of Stonehenge, England, was built by seafaring people who came here as early as 1525 B.C., perhaps even before.

Dubbed "the American Stonehenge" and maintained with great sacrifice by a private New England archaeological research organization called NEARA, this site, nevertheless, stands squarely against conventional assumption by conservative archaeologists, who still look fondly at Columbus, the Norsemen, and perhaps St. Brendan . . . but certainly not at the possibility of ancient Phoenicians and Celt Iberians coming here and erecting observatories.

If this partially excavated ruin is known as "the American Stonehenge" it is more because of its purpose than because it looks like its famous British namesake.

The site is at North Salem, New Hampshire, a few miles

Mystery Hill, North Salem, New Hampshire

from the Massachusetts border, and encompasses twenty acres of ground. Actually, the sanctuary itself occupies the highest part of the hill, but there are signs of building activity reaching for at least two miles in circumference. Recently, additional excavations have shown that the entire hill was used as a very large observatory, with monoliths or dolmens indicating certain positions of the sun. In order to see all that presently remains of the ancient sanctuary, one must walk a considerable distance from the center of it, which indicates that this was by no means a small, local temple, but a major site.

One reaches Mystery Hill by car from Route 111, and follows a winding county-road halfway up the hill. There the road ends in front of a handsome log cabin type house, which is the administration building of the New England Antiquities Research Association, which maintains the site. In this comfortable building there are displays of artifacts unearthed at the site over the years, drawings and maps of reconstructions, and ad display cases of research material and publications pertinent to Mystery Hill. But the building is not only a small museum, it also serves as a kind of country drugstore where visitors can get a cup of tea or a small meal, at least during the summer, and as a souvenir shop, selling not only Mystery Hill stickers and flags, but such diverse items as pine cone incense and miscellaneous trivia donated by friends of the association in order to raise funds for further research.

Everything that is taken in at this place goes toward the one and only goal: to dig further into the site and to restore as much of it as possible to its former appearance. During the summer season there are volunteer guides available who take tourists up to the rest of the hill and explain the various excavations to them.

But in addition to strictly scientific research into the hill's past, I decided to include psychic impressions by reputable psychics, both professionals and amateurs, in my findings: they are here presented for the first time, as *Long Before Columbus* seemed to me not so much a book dealing with psychic work as an archaeological exploration. Among the people I brought up to the hill was a young woman, a "white witch" named Dionysia, her group, and a coven from Boston, ostensibly to celebrate the season on this ancient site.

Everything was set for the circle celebration. However, Doinysia, the high priestess, decided to look at the site by herself to make sure everything was as she would want it to be. She visited Mystery Hill alone, taking the opportunity to use her psychic talents for impressions derived from being among the ruins. I asked her to send me a report, should she obtain any particular psychic reading.

"There are many layers of emotion at this site," she reported, "but the strongest is that of the Celtic builders; second is the native Indians, slaves, and farmers. The first interests me the most, needless to say. It was a temple of worship for a runes using people. Only women inhabited the temple area: a high priestess and oracle, a lesser, and a supreme novice, who lived in the watch house, as they named it. They held animal sacrifices only, and only initiates were allowed to attend the rites. A river, whose course has since changed, lay one or two miles beyond the winter solstice stone. The inhabitants' diet was local fruits and vegetables, fish from the river, and local game. They dressed in fur and lived near the river in long wooden huts. And it was the local citizenry who fed the sacred ones. Approximately fifty percent of the compound has been stolen or not found, including the remains of one of their oracles. The sanctuary was fed with water by a spring near the altar, approximately twenty-five feet away, and the sanctuary was kept foliage-free. Men played a minor role in all rituals. This group died out; they were not killed."

Dionysia then added some symbols which she "perceived" from the period. The symbols, drawn by the high priestess, included a Viking ship, a bunch of four wheat stalks, a pottery bottle, and a deer or antlered animal, and finally, a leaf. She went on to explain her impressions that the Indians took over years later, perhaps nine hundred years ago, and used the place for shelter in the winter. They also lived on the edge of the river but lasted only a short time due to the cold weather, lack of game, and the openness of the area. She then drew a fish, two types of arrows, and a crude arrowhead as belonging to this period. Concerning the third layer, involving slaves and farmers, she thought they were overlapping each other: "I see scared men hiding behind potatoes, running from something. Also many children playing in the sanctuary area."

Unless Dionysia had carefully studied the descriptive material of the Hill, and I have no way to prove or disprove this one way or the other, her observations do contain some surprising elements. Whether Vikings actually came to the Hill or not, we cannot be sure, but if there was an occupation by Irish monks, as Charles Boland believes, these Culdee monks were fleeing from Viking pursuers and presumably the Vikings came after them. The Hill was a prominent landmark in the area and could not very well be overlooked. The drawing of a deer may have something to do with the Ibex found engraved in back of the oracle chamber and the drawings of fish and arrows and the arrowhead are indeed common to the area, not only to Mystery Hill. However, there was nothing in her initial report that was not already public knowledge, whether she had read it or not. Consequently, I suggested that she attempt another psychometry test with me when we had the chance to do so in September.

Since we had arrived in the afternoon, it was decided to attempt psychometry prior to the ceremony itself, which would be undertaken after dinner. I asked Dionysia to lean against the sacrificial stone, and to attempt a psychometric re-creation of its past.

"What sort of people built this place?" I asked.

"They came in long ships, similar to Norse, but with a different prow. The prow was wider, with grotesque figures, more like Japanese or Chinese dragons."

I then asked where the boats came from.

"Somewhere in Scandinavia, I would say about 3000 B.C. They came as colonists. I also think there was a war, but they were colonists," she answered.

"Did they build this temple?"

"Yes, but it was different then from what it is now. Time and people changed it. About ninety percent of them died off. Famine, the severeness of the winter; the survivors intermarried with the Indians."

"Where did these people originally come from?"

"Somehow, I get the idea of Turkey into Scandinavia and then here. Originally from the Mediterranean area, white people."

"Do they have a written language?"

"Yes, but it is an unknown language . . . similar to cuneiform."

"If they came here to build this temple, what was the purpose of it, to which god or goddess was it dedicated?"

"To many gods and goddesses, a pagan temple. There are a number of altars here. I believe originally there were three or four."

"Were there ever any human sacrifices performed on this sacrificial table on which we are now sitting?"

"No, but there were many animal sacrifices. I think this area was the focal point for the main temple. There may have been other temples, but this was the main one. Here the high priest and priestess trained; it was like a school of learning for the public. One of them has the initial A." She then added that rituals performed in the area of the sacrificial table were similar to the "third degree" of Wicca, meaning that they were erotic rituals for fertility purposes.

Dionysia had done some work with me in the psychic field and proven to have a fair degree of ESP. Consequently, I tried to evaluate her reading of the stones from that angle. Discounting her likely conscious knowledge of the area, there were still elements that might have genuine psychometric value. For instance, her stating that the early settlers came from Scandinavia but were not indigenous to that area, adding that they originally came from the Mediterranean, is of some interest. Any ship traveling from the Mediterranean would have made use of prevailing strong currents taking it past Spain and Iceland toward the North American continent. It was just possible that natives of the Mediterranean area might have made way stations in Scandinavia, whether Norway or Iceland, and had thence continued to America. Her remark that the strangers died out about nine hundred years ago would again coincide with the usual dates of the Viking invaders.

Next, I asked one of the young girls of the Boston coven, who had earlier informed me of her psychic abilities and interests, to attempt a psychometric reading. The young lady, aged twenty-two, gave her name as Ben, explained that she was born under the Zodiac sign of Cancer and worked as a secretary in Boston. I asked her for any clairvoyant impressions concerning the age, purpose, and history of Mystery Hill.

"When I was coming up through the woods," Ben replied, "it seemed as if the whole woods was bathed in white light and there was a bluish tinge to it. There was a sort of heavy presence, a very heavy aura over the whole thing. I get the feeling here once in a while of white figures, in white robes, wandering about; they seem to be vanishing around corners, going into a cave, and some of the robes have hoods on them while others do not. The women have very long hair, mostly dark, although there is one that is blond. The men are very dark people, sort of a deep bronze-tan. They look like Indians but they are not Indians, and I get the feeling they came from Atlantis."

I questioned the young lady concerning her interest in Atlantis, and discovered she had read several books on the subject and thought she herself had been incarnated in that ancient world. Consequently, her opinion concerning the derivation of the strangers would have to be seen from that point of view.

"How did these people come here?" I asked.

"They came through the air," Ben replied to my surprise. "It was a round thing, dark-colored, brown or black, made of a strange metal. A flying machine from Atlantis."

"How long ago did this happen?"

"It was during the second upheaval. They decided they wanted to leave and just happened to come here. They were spreading out all over; there had been other groups who left Atlantis before and had gone to different places, but nobody had come in this direction, so they chose it. Accidentally they found this place."

"What was the purpose of this temple?"

"The temple was here before them. It was here when they came. People were here before them."

"Can you tell me anything about the people who were here originally?"

"They were very shadowy; they sort of faded into the forest. They were very close to the forest; you get the feeling they can turn into trees and sort of fade off."

"What deity was it dedicated to?"

"It was a god, but they did not have a name for him. It was a very personal thing. The rituals were very simple."

"Were there any sacrifices?"

"They would sometimes sacrifice a deer they caught, and they did raise deer."

"Do you see any rituals actually taking place, now that you sit on this 'sacrificial table'?"

"I can see a figure—there is white cloth over it and it is lying flat. I think it is a deer and is tied with the horns and the front feet."

"Has any human being been sacrificed on this table?"

"Yes, both men and women, also children. After the Atlantians . . . the Atlantian cult fell into decadence and there were human sacrifices after that."

Carolyn, a tall, young woman of nineteen, who had been a student of Wicca for some time, volunteered next to undergo a psychometric test at the sacrificial table. Naturally, I undertook these tests separately, and none of the three ladies had occasion to hear what the other two had said.

"I have been wandering about, and as I was coming up here it was almost as if I heard music, drums, but not like our skin drums. It starts easy, but then it is almost like a rush when you get here. You can almost see the people, but they are not like us. They are brown-skinned, not as fair as we are, and they have darker hair. The men have beards. They're wearing animal skins, and when they are coming up here, it is almost as if they were racing up the hill. They reach here in a panic and then they cross over and there is a certain point where there is peace."

"Why do you think they are coming here?" I asked.

"It is some important event they have been waiting for, and it is all premeditated. It has to do with this table. After everyone gets here, it is like a Third Degree initiation, a very sacred thing; it's more than that . . . a lot of things have changed. Norse or something, they come and there is peace, and there are five fires lit in rings, and they are out there. They are chanting when they come in, singing a sort of hurrying song. They gather around and there are a high priest and a high priestess. There is a knife, and the high priestess kneels. The high priest kneels and she puts the blade on his chest and on his head and on his shoulders, and then she holds it up and there is a chant. They kiss and then all the people sort of . . . there is a real solemn thing. Then the people go out to where the fires are, beyond the fence."

"What about the priest and priestess? Do they stay behind?"

"Yes, they have a holy union on this rock, no evil, and I have the feeling that this just wasn't an ordinary high priest and high priestess initiated, there was something more special, something greater but I don't know what."

"Who are these people? Where did they come from, and when?" I asked.

"It had to be really long ago, thousands of years. They came from everywhere, because this was a general thing. I think they were European. All I can think of is Druids."

"Were there ever human sacrifices on this stone?"

"Something terrible happened here. Killing and almost a massacre. It was after they set the stone to mark the night that everybody came forth."

"Who massacred them?"

"Soldiers, tall with blond hair. They had green arms and red arms. Helmets and swords. Blades and round shields, they were all the same."

"Did you hear their language?"

"No. But I could hear cries."

"Where the soldiers white?"

"Yes."

Again, a somewhat different story had emerged. Carolyn, of course, knew her Wicca lore; still, she had never been to Mystery Hill before and Bob Stone had not handed out descriptive booklets, so it is reasonable to assume she knew nothing about the history and background of the place. Her description of the drums and ritual seemed original enough, and the massacre by blond men may very well have referred to the clashes between Vikings and Culdees. On the other hand, the Irish emigrants did not wear fur clothes, as far as we know. Perhaps native Indians did, but all this is conjecture.

I chose Friday, the 13th of June, to take a talented young lady by the name of Nancy Abel to New Hampshire. Although Nancy had given ample proof of her psychometric abilities, and had had some ESP experiences through the years, this was her first experience "in the field," and she was understandably nervous.

On arrival on a misty, wet morning, we immediately proceeded to the ruins, and it was agreed that Nancy would roam the site at will, armed only with her psychic talents and a notebook, and would be given time to gather her wits and then report back to me any psychic impressions she might receive. Meanwhile, I set up my motion picture camera, to record additional footage for the documentary I was producing for television.

Her first impression came when we passed the so-called watch house; she approached it, touched it, sat on its stones and then started to write things down furiously. From there she moved on to the sacrificial table where I eventually caught up with her. "At the watch house I felt people were there and they were very tense, looking out for strangers."

"What did you notice further on along the path?"

"There was a pointed rock to the left as we were walking past and I felt it was a grave of some kind." The stone she was referring to was a worked rock opposite the so-called lower well, evidently part of a house or some other form of building which had not yet been explored by the association.

Now it must be kept in mind that Nancy Abel knew nothing about Mystery Hill, had never heard of it, had no opportunity to read anything whatever concerning it, was not shown any literature of the kind so freely handed out to Mr. Senning's sensitives, and had made no attempt to pump me for information on the flight over. What ever came from her lips was therefore totally original—authentic, if you wish—and cannot be ascribed to any previous knowledge.

"I feel someone other than earth people helped these people very much. They were people not from this planet. I received this impression while I was sitting on that rock."

I asked Nancy what impression she received of people connected with the site itself.

"They were definitely intelligent people, prehistory as we would think of it. Not American Indians or primitives, but quite intelligent. That was a long time ago." Nancy seemed fascinated with the sacrificial table; she sat down on it, crossed-legged, writing things down—at one point, seemingly half out of her body, with her eyes not focusing properly.

Eventually, she got up and came toward me. "I feel that being from other planets were worshipped on that table," she said. "I can see someone sitting on that table from another planet talking to the people here, or trying to talk to them, as if to help them out. I get the impression of someone with eyes pointed like that, long elongated eyes. Compared to us this being is short, the skin is olive-colored. Now I am trying to see where the people are, they were all around here while this being talked."

I asked her to keep the vision within her mind, and to describe, as much as possible, what this being looked like. She closed her eyes and continued her narrative.

"It is a man; I see he has a belt, I don't know if he has much clothes on, but I see a belt and something around his arm, a band. I don't see any hair on his head. He's wearing shoes."

I asked her what the man's face looked like.

"The nose seems completely flat, I only see two nostrils, two holes to breathe. The mouth is sort of round, rather than having the shape we know."

I had an afterthought and asked her to look at the man's belt again.

"There is something on that belt, but I can't make it out. I think it is something to communicate with."

"What is he saying to the people here?"

"I don't thing they understand him. He seems to be communicating with them through telepathy. However, they do understand his messages, but they are also confused as to who he is; he doesn't make sense to them."

"Is he here alone?"

"He is alone," she said, "but I think there may be one or two more."

I asked Nancy to focus on the people watching the strange being. What did they look like?

"They look like typical primitive men, not wearing any shoes, all crouched together, looking intently at the being and wondering whatever he might be doing here. They are wearing very primitive clothes, the kind a caveman would wear. I saw lots of fur. Their skin is the same as ours."

"What was this stone on which the man landed used for?"

"They worshipped from here when he wasn't around. I think they made offerings to him from here. I don't think they hurt their own people, but they did make some sort of sacrifice. They used human sacrifices, at least that is what I get from it."

I asked her whether she heard anything, but she explained that the being from another planet was speaking silently, as it were, and as for the people watching the stranger—"I heard mango . . . I heard the *sh* syllable, with a lot of it. I think if it has to sound similar to any language we know, it sounds African. There are a lot of words with *sh* in them."

Bob Stone and his cousin, Osborn Stone, joined us now and we began to walk around the site, stopping here and there, and eventually tracing the outer circuit, stopping at the various markers and solstice stones in order to give Nancy a chance to pick up psychic imprints.

I asked her how old she thought the site was. At first, she didn't know what to say.

"My feeling is that when you go to school and study anthropology, well this is before you start studying about man even existing."

We were now walking toward the summer solstice stone, away from the main site. Suddenly she stopped and said, "I just had a different impression of people who dressed differently. They are still barefoot, but I see this woman wearing a thin dress, close-fitting, either very light orange or white in color. It comes to the knee or even above the knee. The woman has long hair; she is very pretty and she is walking alone. I think she is going to the water, something to do with the water there. This is a completely different impression from what I got when I was on the rocks. These are different people; I just wonder if they existed at the same time. But even these people, I feel, have something to do with the being from another plant."

I went over her remarks once again, making sure that what she had said was true: three layers, the primitive people in fur, the woman in the gown, and the being from outer space. She agreed that was what she had felt. "I feel it was a landing site, there were more aboard ship, but one came out to meet the people and I think it was there at the sacrificial table. But I think it landed behind that rock, in the area down there." She pointed toward a clearing there, large enough even today for a UFO to land.

"Why did they come to Mystery Hill?"

"I think there was a war. I don't know if these people survived it, and whether they came down to help, but I feel there were only a few people left from something before. This war was on earth but I don't know where it was. The people here were the survivors from it and the other being was trying to help them to start all over again."

We had now arrived at a stone wall extending in either direction into the woods. It seemed like a perimeter of some sort, but Bob Stone assured me that it did not go all the way around, that, in fact, none of the walls were round or oval, but went in every direction for a certain distance and then stopped just as abruptly as they had begun. Thus far the association had not established any pattern followed by the builders of these walls, and the reason for their existence remained a puzzle. "What happens is that you walk along this wall and you can see there are big stones in it periodically as if to mark something," Stone explained. "Evidently, they used different stations to observe. I think this was an observation post." We continued our walk around the site until we came to the winter solstice stone. Bob Stone explained that they had found a total of thirty-eight walls, of various lengths.

Osborn Stone suggested we continue walking down to a stone with markings known as the so-called G markings. It was some distance from where we were, but he thought it was worth the descent. Beyond it lay the steep cliff where Indian

Mystery Hill

Photos by Hans Holzer

pottery had been unearthed for years. Despite the wet grass and the underbrush, we followed Osborn Stone as he led the way to the stone with the G markings. As I saw it from close up, I realized that the man-made incision was not the letter G at all, but a combination of three, or perhaps four, characters. We continued on to another stone called the moon stone, northwest of the main site. One could clearly see that a face had been engraved in the upper right corner and it reminded one of the traditional "man in the moon." Nancy touched it and said, "It makes me feel there are beings from other worlds here."

We continued to a stone with another carved face on it; Bob Stone pointed out that the face had slanted eyes, unlike any human face known on earth. Even though the stone had suffered from exposure to the weather, it was obviously a human face that had been carved into it. Was this a portrait of the stranger from space, carved by the people living at the site? So many questions remained unanswered.

Nancy, unaccustomed to the emotional tension of psychic adventure, felt tired, and we called it a day, especially as it was getting dark. After a good night's rest, we returned to the site in the morning. Despite the presence of a considerable amount of mosquitoes, Nancy was walking around the hill, paying renewed attention to the sacrificial table and walking in and out of the oracle chamber with a thoughtful expression on her face. Eventually she joined Bob and Osborn Stone and me and, looking at her notes, began to comment on what she had experienced this morning.

"As far as the sacrificial table is concerned," she began, "I feel there were two periods, two different groups of people from two periods in time. At the later time there were animal sacrifices. Also, I didn't see any men, I saw only women, and they were making sacrifices to nature, not to any being. They were dressed just as I saw them yesterday, that one beautiful woman in very thin clothing. It was Grecian. When I was in the oracle chamber, I felt blood, I felt part of the ceremony went on down there. I think they made sacrifices, and the remains of the animals slain on the table were taken down underneath, and I felt that they were either eating them or burning the rest of it."

"What is the order, in time, of the three layers?" I asked her.

"The one from space came to the original people here, and then, after the original people weren't around anymore, then these other women came wearing these gowns, afterward," Nancy replied. "I have the feeling that the second group of people were chased away by some form of war."

We barely made the noon plane back to New York. The sun had meanwhile come out, as if to wish us a somewhat ironic farewell, as we had hoped for it all along. On the way back I got to thinking about Nancy's contribution to the Mystery Hill research, and that of my earlier meetings. I had visited the Hill in the company of three psychic individuals, Ethel Johnson Myers, a lady who had been a professional trance medium for years; Ingrid Beckman, a young woman in her late twenties, whom I have trained for the past three or four years; and Nancy Abel, a beginner with promising psychic talent. All three had said certain things that matched, yet all three had no way of knowing about these things. From their testimony, and that of the psychic individuals who had been to the hill earlier, when I first visited it, a sort of composite picture began to emerge.

All psychics had agreed that several different races or people had occupied Mystery Hill. All had agreed that the American Indians had nothing to do with it. All felt the site had been occupied a long time ago, prior to what we are commonly taught is prehistory. What they picked up from the atmosphere of the place, what had remained in the immediate surroundings of the place, were nothing more than human emotions, frozen in time, tiny electrical impulses left behind and coating the rocks upon which the actual tragedies had been played out. All three psychics saw a short, dark-skinned race, a tall, fair-skinned race of superior beings, and incursions from outside earth. All three spoke of Greek elements being present, and if we take the term Greek in its broadest sense, that is to say, pre-Hellenic Greece, we must include what we have come to call Phoenicians and Cretans, or Minoans. Interestingly, none of the psychics felt the presence of Norsemen, and even less of the fabled Irish Culdees. Fortunately, the establishment scientists are slowly but surely coming around to the idea that ancient people did indeed settle in America.

The late Professor Barry Fell of Harvard, one of America's top experts in ancient writings, said, "There is absolutely no doubt about it. I found three inscriptions at the temple. They were in Celtic, a European language. And by comparing them to other Celtic inscriptions found in Portugal, I was able to date them back to between 800 and 600 B.C."

Dr. Fell was able to translate the inscriptions found at Mystery Hill as "dedicated to the sun god Bel." Another inscribed stone, found at the same site, reads, "Embellished by . . . cut this stone." Dr. Fell pointed out that Mystery Hill showed strong similarities with England's Stonehenge. Four giant stone slabs are strategically placed exactly where the sun rises and sets on the longest and shortest day of the year, June 21st and December 21st. Dr. Fell is quoted he was "convinced that we now have sufficient evidence to show that an advanced culture existed in America as far back as three thousand years ago. But as to how it got here, that is still a mystery."

When Dr. Fell speaks of Celtic people, we should realize we are not thinking in terms of today's Celts (i.e., Irish, Scottish, Welsh) but rather the Ibero–Celts who originally came from the Eastern Mediterranean: in other words, people from Greek areas, such as Minoan Crete and pre-Semitic Phoenicia. The "Celtic" sun god Bel, of whom Dr. Fell speaks, is really no other than the Phoenician Bal.

Index

About the Author

Han Holzer, Ph.D., is the author of 131 books, including *Ghosts, ESP and You, The Handbook of Parapsychology, The Power of Hypnosis, Are You Psychic,* and *Life Beyond.* He taught parapsychology for eight years at the New York Institute of Technology, and was educated at Columbia University, the University of Vienna, and received a doctorate from the London College of Applied Science.

Dr. Holzer has also been an active television and film writer, producer, and on-camera person, notably for the NBC series *In Search Of . . .* and half a dozen documentaries. He has surveyed the psychic scene, and developed a number of gifted psychics for many years. He makes his home in New York City.